THE WEDDING SURVIVAL GUIDE

by Catherine Balavage

Copyright 2014

ISBN- 978-150-3266339

First published in December 2014

INTRODUCTION.

The Wedding Survival Guide: How To Plan Your Big Day Without Losing Your Sanity.

Congratulations! You're engaged. Enjoy this moment. Getting engaged is a magical thing and everyone you know will be as happy as you are. Well, mostly.... You will keep staring at your ring, and that's okay. So is flashing it, and posting pictures of it on Instagram, Facebook and Twitter. You may worry about being obnoxious, and you may even slip slightly into that territory but this is your moment. Getting engaged is a (hopefully) once-in-a-lifetime experience. Let yourself fully enjoy the moment. The people who love you will understand and also probably act that way when they get engaged too. Let yourself enjoy the moment without embarrassment.

When I got engaged I put something tentatively on Facebook and then promised everyone that I would shut up now. Next came comments from my amazing friends, 'Are you kidding? You're engaged. Milk this moment for everything it's worth!'. So follow my friends' advice and allow yourself to become fully and happily immersed in the moment. Especially as getting engaged is the happy, easy part of the entire thing. Next, up comes the wedding planning....

According to the UK Alliance of Wedding Planners these are the average costs of various weddings:

Venue & Catering : £9,500

Photography: £2,100

Flowers: £1,200

Entertainment : £1,220

Bridal dress, shoes, veil and groom's outfit : £1,680

Total, including other costs: £21,000

It may help to know that you are not alone. In the UK alone about a quarter of a million couples get married every year and on average they pay a whopping twenty-one thousand pounds for the privilege. Once it has sunk in the first thing to decide is when you are going to get married. Some people have long engagements and others get married quickly. Of course there will be a number of factors that help you decide. You may need to save so will wait a while, you may be pregnant and have a shotgun wedding (nothing wrong with that), you might want to get married in a specific season or just want to get married as soon as possible. Next you will want to put together a guest list. DO NOT TELL ANYONE THEY ARE INVITED YET. This is important. Weddings are expensive and the more people you have, the more expensive they are. Some people will rudely assume they are invited, just gently tell them that you have not done the guest list yet and if they are not invited then also point out that you are having a small wedding.

The first thing to do is decide on a rough date and year, after that you can start finding a venue. They will want possible dates obviously, and some book up years in advance. The venue is the building block, you can put everything else together after you have found the perfect one. I was originally going to call this book How To Plan The Perfect Wedding Without Breaking The Bank. It is still full of budget-saving tips and ideas but after my own wedding was over I realised that what I wish I had had was a survival guide. People will have different budgets and some lucky people will also have family members contributing. My fiancé and I were one of those: thank you family! But no matter your budget I am here to help and hold your hand. I am going to tell you everything I learned from planning my own wedding, everything I learned from the experts and all of the information I have gathered from my research. I have tried to cover everything and I have tried to give as much value to the book as possible. In short: I have tried to make it the book that would have saved me all of the stress and waste of time and money. I hope you enjoy it and you have the most amazing, magical wedding day.

What can go wrong...

There were a lot of things I thought might go wrong on my wedding day: a massive spot, a broken shoe, forgetting something, being late...in fact when it came to my wedding (almost) everything that could go wrong went wrong. The groom was so ill we never thought we would actually be able to get married. We even spent the night before the wedding in A&E, got home at 3:30am, got a few hours' sleep and then the first thing my (then) fiancé said to me was, 'I don't know if I can get married today.' Argh!

After a quick trip to the doctor for an emergency appointment and some prescription pills my wonderful groom managed to pull himself together through a sheer show of strength and willpower. He managed until after the speeches and then back off to the hospital we went!

But here is the thing: people loved our wedding. Apart from a sick groom and being late because my father wasn't ready (yes, you read that right. The only bride who was late for her own wedding because her father hadn't finished getting ready), our wedding went perfectly. Sure there were a few things that weren't perfect but many people said that the wine and the food was the best wedding wine and food they ever tasted, they loved the venue, the flowers...everything. The fact is, many things will go wrong but what people really will remember is how much fun they had and how great the day was. Just take the disasters in your stride and know that sometimes perfection is sometimes imperfect. You will even be able to laugh about it further down the line. Comedy is tragedy plus time. As long as you manage to get married pretty much everything else will be fine. People will enjoy themselves and everyone will be on your side. Don't stress because things will go wrong but it won't matter as much as you think it does. Just take it in your stride, knowing that you have now gained a new spouse and that today is the first day of your new life together. Disasters only add to the spirit of the day and make people pull together.

CHAPTER 1: GETTING STARTED

Sometimes getting started is the most daunting part and weddings are no exception. I had no idea where to start, just a long list of things that needed done. There is no need to panic however, because here is a timeline checklist.

YOUR TIMELINE CHECKLIST

While all weddings are different, there will be some things that are the same for each one. Here is a handy timeline checklist to help keep you on track. Some of the timing may be different, don't panic!, this is just to keep you on track. There is a lot to do but try to have fun and enjoy. This is a one-in-a-lifetime experience.

12-8 MONTHS

Announce your engagement. Lots of people now do this on Facebook but keep in mind that some close family members will be upset if they find out this way.

Decide what type of ceremony you want. You can have a civil or a religious ceremony.

Set a Date. Discuss with your fiancé what dates are good. Think about what season you want to get married in. Summer is popular but autumn and winter weddings are just as beautiful. Getting married in summer is also more expensive as it is peak wedding season.

Set a budget. This will help when you come to do your guest list and book your venue. Working with the budget you have is very important to stop it spiraling out of control. Stick to your budget as much as possible. It is easy to see your wedding as a once-in-a-lifetime experience and go crazy thinking this is a one-off day that you will remember for the rest of your life. Well, it is a once-in-a-lifetime experience that you will remember for the rest of your life but not because of the napkins or the favours: what you will remember is marrying the love of your life and how wonderful it was to have all of your favourite people in the one room at the same time. It is not the superficial things that make a wedding, but the people involved.

Start creating a guest list. Apart from close friends and family who will definitely be there, do not let anyone know they are invited yet. You may have to cut your budget or decide you did not want that person there after all. The key thing here is to not just invite everyone you have ever met. I will say this a lot in this book: weddings are expensive! Every single person will cost you a lot of money. Don't just invite 'friends' you haven't even seen in years who only contact you when they want something or the cousin who has always been horrible to you and makes you feel miserable. It is your wedding day and if people get upset that they were not invited then tough. If you do value someone's friendship however then do invite them. If you do not invite someone to your wedding and they thought you were a close

friend it will very probably ruin your friendship unless you make it very clear that you are just having a small, intimate wedding which is mostly just family.

Decide on bridesmaids, maid of honour, best man and ushers. Then tell them. They will delighted. Hopefully.

Send Save The Date cards or email/call people to let them know the date. I think emailing is fine and then send out proper paper invites about six weeks before.

Research and book your wedding venue. hitched.com is particularly good for this. Just put in the area where you live and loads of venues will be listed. You can then email them or request a brochure. This is how I found our wedding venue, the London Rowing Club. I knew immediately it was 'The One'. It goes without saying that you should see a wedding venue before you book it.

Book your photographer and videographer. Do your research and try to get feedback from people they have worked with before.

Consider whether to get **wedding insurance**. We didn't but our wedding wasn't very expensive.

Book your honeymoon. The earlier you book, the cheaper it will be.

Find the perfect dress. This is the fun part. I bought my wedding dress with my mother, father and even my brother and fiancé were there. My fiancé didn't see the dress as he is very superstitious but my mother cried, my dad had a tear in his eye and even my brother said I looked amazing. For many bridal boutiques you will have to book an appointment to see the dresses. Some even charge a fee as high as £50. Be fussy about ones that charge, especially if it is a lot of money. It will add up.

Research accommodation for guests near the venue if you are getting married in the country or abroad. It is a gesture that will be greatly appreciated.

Book florist. They will be able to tell you which flowers are in season. A good florist will be a great help.

Book caterer. The earlier the better.

Book band or DJ.

Pick your wedding colours. More important than you think. Will be needed for buying the flowers and doing the decoration.

Book a makeup artist and hair stylist if you are having one.

Book a Master of Ceremonies if you need one and the venue does not provide one. You could get a family member to do this too. Sometimes the personal touch really works.

7-5 MONTHS

Order invitations and other wedding stationery. We got our amazing wedding invitations on eBay.

Order wedding cake.

Book transportation.

Get outfits for wedding party.

Order wedding rings.

Set up your own wedding website if you want.

Consider buying new honeymoon wardrobe.

Choose and buy venue decoration.

Choose and buy wedding favours.

Organise the date for the hen and stag do with friends. After this leave it to them to plan it. I now have the best piece of advice I can possibly give: *do not have the stag/hen do the weekend before the wedding.* Nor the week before the wedding. Do it TWO WEEKS before the wedding at least. I begged my husband and his friends to have the stag do two weeks before but no one listened and I ended up spending my wedding night in A&E, in my wedding dress. It was not an enjoyable experience and at one point I even almost got sectioned as they thought I was just some random woman walking around wearing a wedding dress. If you take nothing else from this book, at least take this. You may also want to point out to your fiancé and his friends that you don't have to get completely smashed to have a good time. (To be fair to my husbands' friends he did have two stag nights and was stressed.)

4-2 MONTHS

Print menus and order of service. Watch out for any spelling mistakes.

Finalise menu with caterer.

Order alcohol. We got ours from a wonderful villa in Tuscany. It wasn't as expensive as it sounds.

Send out invites and make sure they have information on venue, accommodation, transportation and your gift list information.

Choose and order flowers.

Make sure your passports are valid.

Register and do your gift list.

Check times and any other details with your suppliers.

Decide on readings, music and hymns with registrar/officiant.

Organise your banns if getting married in a church.

Meet with registrar and go over vows and order of service.

Start working on speeches.

1 MONTH TO GO.

Buy gifts for bridesmaids and the rest of the wedding party.

Have final fittings and arrange date to pick up outfits.

Make sure you are not missing anything important: shoes, garter, veil, tights/stockings, underwear or cufflinks, shirt and shoes for groom.

Inform wedding party members of their duties for the day. Let them know what will happen and send over an order of service.

Buy guestbook and any final touches.

Confirm final numbers with caterers. Make sure you send along any dietary requirements of guests.

Do your seating plan.

Send out invitations.

Book hair and makeup trial.

Organise any extra entertainment. If there will be children coming you may want a children's table with fun activities to keep them entertained.

Make sure you **get any injections** you will need for your honeymoon.

Finalise details with all of your suppliers. Confirm all bookings.

Write down all of the details of your suppliers and any other people involved in your wedding and then give it to a member of the wedding party in case anything goes wrong and people need to be chased up.

Buy or make wedding favours.

Finalise your wedding playlist and make sure the last dance song and any other instructions are clearly stated. Also mark out ceremony music and cake cutting music. Our uncle Matthew played the lute at our wedding and not only was he amazing but it added a truly wonderful and unique touch. If you have a friend or family member who is a talented musician then ask them if they will play during the ceremony or maybe do a set or two? It could be your wedding present from them and they will probably be flattered you asked.

Finalise your speeches. Practice will help too. It is quite nerve-wracking making a speech.

Finalise the order of service.

Make or buy place cards.

Book first night hotel.

Book any beauty treatments.

Arrange for a friend or member of the wedding party to **return any rented items**.

THE FINAL WEEK.

Panic. Only kidding.

Pick up your **wedding dress**.

Pay everyone who needs paying.

Finalise the seating plan.

The Wedding Survival Guide

Wear in wedding shoes.

Pack for the **honeymoon**.

Clean your engagement ring.

Have a once over everything.

And if you want to be super organised…**write the thank you cards** for wedding gifts that have been ordered. This will take the pressure off post-wedding and people will be impressed at how speedy you were.

Put together an emergency kit of painkiller, mini-hairspray, tights, pins, mints, makeup and anything else you can think of.

The Night Before

Decorate the venue if you are required to do so.

Drop off the alcohol and any other supplies at the venue.

Make sure you are all packed for the honeymoon. Don't forget the passports!

Get or give yourself a **manicure**.

Check over everything. Make sure that both of your outfits are complete. Check your shoes and accessories too.

And relax. Have a bath or just spend some time together. Watch a comedy or cook. Then have an early night. It is exciting but try to get some sleep.

Should You Get Married?

Now you have a handy countdown let's start with the most important thing first: should you be getting married? I know, Why is this in a wedding book? Some people get married for the wrong reasons and other people get married even though they know something is wrong. Read below and go through my checklist to find out when and if you should be getting married.

So, when is it the right time to get married and make that commitment? What do you need to know first? Read the points below to find out if now is the right time to get married.

Are you in love?
There are many reasons why people think they should get married. Whether it's peer pressure or because you have kids. Truth is, there is only one reason why you

should get married: You're in love. As long as you love someone it does not matter what life throws at you. They are the constant in your life. If you are unsure whether

or not you're in love; you're not. If you are unsure if your boyfriend loves you, ask him or read this: How to tell if your boyfriend loves you

Are they your final emotional destination?
When you marry someone you are not just sharing your life, but also your soul and your DNA. You are forever joining together. Marriage is something to be taken seriously. Do you really want to be with this person? It's okay to have doubts, we all do. It is always possible that Angelina Jolie or George Clooney will want to marry you later, but the thing is, if you have found someone who loves you and you love them back you are blessed, people spend lifetimes trying to find the love of their lives. Don't throw that away.

Are you just sliding into it?
Do you really want to get married or are you just sliding into it? Marriage is a mistake that's hard to get out of unscathed – whether that be emotionally or financially. Being in a loveless marriage is something nobody should have to put up with. Don't just get married because your mother is nagging you.

Do you just want a big day?
They say the most important day in a women's life is her wedding day. I like to think this isn't true, but it is still something women (and men!) buy into. After the dress, the presents and the honeymoon you will have to spend the rest of your life with this person. Not really worth one glamorous day.

Are you getting married because you (think) you are cracking on a bit?
Getting married because you're nearly thirty isn't a good enough reason. Although a woman's biological clock doesn't work in her favour, marrying someone you don't love – or worse, having a kid with someone you don't love; a child ties you to that person forever- just because you feel pressure from society or your parents will never make you happy. Think of all the other things you could do with your life; travel, focus on your career, study. There is a big world out there. You don't need a husband (or wife) for that.

Do you know each other? Does the other person listen?
You have to know the person you are marrying. Can you communicate with them? Can you talk openly? If you tell your partner that something annoys you do they make the effort to change? If someone loves you they will do anything they can to keep you around, they will care about your thoughts and feelings. You also have to accept the other person, good and bad.

And another thing…

Talk about finance, children and future goals together. It's okay to be nervous, to be unsure, relationships are hard, but if you really love the person you are with, what are you waiting for?

This was the first entry from my wedding diary on my online magazine Frost Magazine:

Well I finally did it. I managed to find someone who will put up with me for the rest of my life. Most little girls' dream came true when my boyfriend of three years whisked me off to Paris on the Eurostar for our anniversary and proposed. I ecstatically said Yes and upon our return bought far too many wedding magazines, and realised just how hard planning a

wedding was going to be. Don't get me wrong. I am not exactly phased by planning big things. I planned the launch party for Frost Magazine and had over 300 guests. It went off without a hitch even though the venue canceled on us a few days before. I have also made a full length feature film. I have the skills and the staying power but what I don't have is £21,000 to spend on a party. Only one person has mentioned the outdated thing of the woman's parents paying. All of my friends paid for their own weddings and I am not asking my parents for money. I am the editor of this magazine, a freelance writer and actor. I am not exactly rolling in it.

Somehow this is not even the issue. Neither my fiancé nor I think it is reasonable to spend that amount of money on one day of your life. Other difficulties are that my family live in Scotland and my fiancé's family live in England. Getting all of these people together in a convenient, reasonably priced venue doesn't feel like the easiest thing.

Also as a half catholic, half protestant agnostic I have found out that I cannot even get married in a church because I was not christened as my parents, quite rightly, wanted me to choose my own religion. If I want to get married in a church I will have to attend church or do a course. Neither of these seem appealing and I don't have a lot of free time.

So join me on my journey from engaged woman to bride. I will be writing lots of wedding articles and advice to go along with my personal experience. Please comment and tell me your thoughts and give any advice. We are planning to get married in June of next year so we don't actually have much time to get everything done. It is all quite exciting and scary. Frost Magazine has a brilliant article on buying the perfect engagement ring if you want to send it to your boyfriend to drop some hints.

THE RINGS.

The engagement ring and the wedding rings. These are very important as you will wear them for the rest of your life. They are also a major purchase as they are very expensive so it really matters that you get it right.

My husband wrote the amazing piece below on choosing an engagement ring. He really did his research and knows his stuff. Have a read.

Buying the perfect diamond engagement ring is not easy. There are serious hurdles to navigate and hopefully this article will help you with some of them. You're about to spend a serious amount of money you need to keep her happy, remember she's going to be wearing this thing for the rest of her life but you also don't want to get ripped off!

How much should you spend?

The first thing to remember with this is that everyone will try to bully you into spending as much money as possible. No matter how much you're actually planning to spend you will be made to feel like it's not enough. Walk into a jewellers planning to spend £5000 and they will gently make you feel as though your budget is inadequate and encourage you to spend more. Magazines will insist that you spend a minimum of three months' salary. The industry is very cleverly set up to make you spend as much as possible. Don't feel pressured. Set a budget on what you're happy to spend and stick with it. Remember you've got a wedding to pay for! If she loves you she will love the ring no matter what. If

she's the sort of woman who checks the size of the ring before saying yes or no she's not worth marrying in the first place. That all being said no one likes a cheapskate so a £10 ring from a supermarket is not going to cut it so keep reading.

Online or Not Online?

I love to make savings buying stuff online but diamond engagement rings are a definite exception. Every stone looks different and you must see it in person before you buy it, no picture will ever tell the story so forget about buying online. It also will sound very unromantic when your fiancée asks where you bought the ring and you're forced to tell her it's from online.

With Her or Without Her?

If you're worried about making a mistake you can buy a plain band for when you propose and then buy the ring with her so you can be sure you get one she likes. There are advantages and disadvantages to this. The advantage is you can be sure she gets what she wants.

The disadvantage is that you're going to have to fork out if she falls in love with a ring. It also makes it much harder to negotiate when the jeweller knows you really want something. Proposing with a plain ring is also not as special and may detract from the moment.

Research
Doing your research is vital of you don't want to make a mistake. It will mean you get the right ring and it could save you a fortune. The more you know the easier its going to be to negotiate and the more a jeweller will respect you.

Understanding the Four Cs

The look and value of a diamond is determined by four factors. Cut, Clarity, Carat and Colour

Cut

The cut is the only characteristic not determined by nature. A poorly cut diamond may have a compromised sparkle. The most common type of cut is the 'round cut'. In my opinion the traditional round cut or variations of it are by far the best cut because they sparkle the

most, a lot more for example than the princess cut. However you should see all the cuts before making a decision. Types of cut include the the emerald, the pear, the marquise, the princess, the oval and the heart shape.

Clarity

The clarity is how perfectly the diamond has been formed in nature. Yes, very few diamonds are perfectly flawless most will have little flaws which you can see under a

magnifying glass. These flaws are called inclusions. Inclusions have a big impact on the value of a diamond

The grading of clarity according to the GIA (Gemological Institute of America)
IF – Internally Flawless
VVS1 and VVS2 Very very slightly included inclusions which are very difficult to see even under 10x magnification
VS1 and VS2 – Very Slightly Included – Difficult to see under 10x magnification
SI1 and SI2 – Slightly Included – Easy for a trained grader to see under 10x magnification
I1, I2 – Included obvious inclusions usually visible to the naked eye
I3 – Large inclusions that typically impact the fire of the diamond and potentially threaten the structure of the stone

Inclusions are a big part of why you need to see a diamond in person. Inclusions can affect the sparkle or fire of a diamond. Sometimes a diamond which has a higher grade may actually have a bigger impact on sparkle than a lower grade. People can make too bigger deal about inclusions. Remember a diamond's inclusions make it unique. Personally I think the money you would spend to buy a VS diamond would be better spent on carat or colour. You should however try to avoid severe inclusions which might compromise a stone's sparkle or structure. This is a personal choice and you must find for yourself what you want but I think the SI categories often offers the best value. Remember though that two diamonds from the same category might look completely different. You must judge how the stone looks.

Colour

The most valuable and rare diamonds are colourless and are graded D. The colour scale runs from D to Z. Diamonds with a very distinct colour are rare and are called fancies. Diamonds typically get more yellowish as you move down the scale. Colour is important but again it is not something I would obsess over as long as you get a reasonable grade. You or your fiancée are not going to tell the difference between an F and an H. In my opinion I would suggest you can probably go up to a J without really having much idea that your diamond was slightly yellow. For me an I or H rating represent the best value but again these are all personal opinions. You might find that for you only a D or E grade will do. Remember every stone is different: trust your eyes, don't just focus on the grades.

Carat

The Carat or the weight and therefore size of the diamond. Not to be confused with karats the purity measure for gold. The carat has a big effect on value and is the first thing everyone will notice. As the size of the carat increases the price grows exponentially. Most diamonds for engagement rings fall between 0.25-2 carats. You will want to get as big a carat as you can within your budget without compromising too much on the other Cs. Don't believe everything you're told by jewellers when it comes to carat. For example they may say to you on that budget you won't be able to buy a carat bigger than X. I was initially shown much smaller diamonds than the one I was eventually able to buy.

Certified or Uncertified

A certified stone is a diamond that has been assessed, graded and coded with a laser by an independent gemological laboratory. The most well-known and recognised is GIA. Other popular certificates include HRD, IGL, EGL and AGS. The disadvantage of an uncertified stone is that you are trusting the jeweller. However a cert stone is usually a few hundred pounds more expensive. A cert stone will also ensure you have not been sold a fake. If you are buying a very expensive stone having a cert stone is probably worth it. If you have a smaller budget you may prefer to risk going without a cert stone. The decision must be yours. Diamonds can be artificially treated or fracture filled and sold legally although you must be told. Avoid these and avoid anything which is 'clarity enhanced'.

Looking Out for Fakes

The Ring Itself

The most common rings today seem to be from white gold and platinum which both look quite similar. You can also go for a yellow gold or a white and yellow gold mix although personally I prefer the platinum or white gold look. Platinum is slightly more expensive than 18 karat white gold. Try and go for at least 18 karats if you can, no one wants 9 karat gold for an engagement ring. Remember 9 karat gold is just 37.5% pure compared to 75% for 18 karat. If they can keep a secret try and glean information from your fiancée's family and friends as to what her taste is. You can differentiate your ring by choosing a variety of different settings although the diamond solitaire is the most common. If you can, try to find out what size ring she takes from her friends or family. If you can't, don't worry too much any reputable jeweller will allow you to get it refitted although this may cost extra.

BUYING THE DIAMOND RING

Where to Buy?

First of all set aside at least half a day. Don't buy a ring in a rush. Do not buy from a high street jeweller you will almost certainly get ripped off and you will have limited choice. If you can try to go to an area where there are a lot of jewellers in one place. Hatton Gardens in London is the best place to go. There are at least 30 jewellers next to each other. You can be assured of competition and a wide choice. Most of the jewellers also have good reputations.

Don't Get Sucked In

The Wedding Survival Guide

First go around every store and check the windows to get an idea. People will probably come out and try and get you to come inside. Talk to them to get more information if you want but don't go inside yet. Try and work out which shops are offering the best deals.

Bear in mind that jewellers will display their best and usually most expensive wares. They will usually have more inside the store. Take pictures of any rings which catch your eye and move on.

When you're ready choose a ring which you like. Go into the store and ask to have a look at it. Here's where you can make use of all that research you've done. Ask the jeweller about the cut, carat etc. Ask to see the ring under 10x jeweller's loupe and on a white background (a black background can hinder the eyes perception of a diamond's colour). Ask if the ring is certified and who did the grading. Remember that an uncertified ring is not

necessarily a bad thing and will usually mean a cheaper ring but is something you need to be aware of. Ask the jeweller what guarantees and warranties they offer.
Then ask if the jeweller has any similar rings to compare it to. All this will make it clear to the jeweller that you know what you're talking about and it will make it easier to negotiate later. Don't be afraid to take your time. Choose the ring which you like the most and ask the jeweller for his best price on that ring. Thank the jeweller, make a note of the details of the ring and tell him/her you'll be back if you don't find anything better. Also remember to ask the jeweller about re-sizing costs, the setting and the material of the actual ring.
Go into the next shop and repeat until you have a really good picture of what's available and you know what you want.

How to Negotiate

Negotiating can be uncomfortable but you absolutely must do it. Remember they are the ones profiting from you and you have the power to go elsewhere. A general rule is to get at least 15%-20% off the list price at a minimum. Don't seem too keen if you really want a particular ring.

A good first move is to ask the jeweller what his or her best price is. That should be your starting point for negotiations. Use your budget as a negotiating tool. When you've clinched the deal remember to get a receipt and remember to ask about fittings. Try to get one for free if you can.

You may also want to read this excellent guide to buying engagement rings from the Guardian. (www.guardian.co.uk/lifeandstyle/2002/feb/13/shopping.familyandrelationships1)

Good Luck!

Conflict/Blood diamonds

In recent years conflict diamonds have become a concern. There is something called the Kimberly Process Certification scheme that was launched in January 2003. It is an international agreement to eliminate the trade in blood diamonds. Blood diamonds are did monds that are used to finance civil wars and other conflicts. It is worth asking your jeweller about this.

You don't need to go for a diamond ring of course. You could have a sapphire, emerald, ruby or anything else that takes your fancy.

Wedding Rings.

This is where women get to put a ring on it too. Trust me, there is nothing sexier than seeing the man you love wearing the wedding ring you bought him. Funnily enough, men didn't really wear wedding rings until after World War II. Hmm. The man's wedding ring is usually a wider version of the women's ring. However this does not need to be the case. I chose a wedding ring with diamonds and sapphires in. My mother had a diamond and sapphire engagement ring and I always loved it. I didn't know what kind of wedding ring I wanted until we went to Hatton Gardens and I fell in love with the one we bought. My husband got a very good deal on my wedding ring and you should always negotiate. Never accept the first price. Ever.

For my husband's wedding ring we went online. We went around a lot of jewellers and he found out exactly what he wanted. However, none of them would budge on the price unless you were buying both wedding rings together. Luckily he got the exact same ring he wanted online for a much better price.

You could also get an inscription on your rings. Some jewellers will even do it for free. 'Put it back on' is a good one.

Most jewellers are reputable but do watch out for any scams. You can get the ring certified by a professional if you are unsure. The jeweller shouldn't mind. Some insurers won't insure your jewellery without an appraisal so that is something to consider.

Traditionally, wedding rings go on the fourth finger of the left hand.

PICKING THE MAID OF HONOUR AND BEST MAN.

This may be hard if you have a lot of friends but do choose wisely. The person who you choose should be organised, responsible and, above all, reliable. Choosing your oldest friend is a good idea and if you have a best friend it is a no-brainer. My husband chose two best men. I chose a maid of honour and a best man. Two of my best friends. The best man did not do anything as he is very busy and I did not want to put any pressure on him but my maid of honour, Paloma, was a godsend. My husband chose well with this best men. The main one was Tom as George was out of the country at the time. Tom, like Paloma, was a godsend. He was incredibly helpful and always gave his honest opinion. We both really appreciated his help and advice. He also had some great ideas that we loved.

You could also choose more than one maid of honour or best man if you really cannot decide. However, many people will just be delighted to be chosen as a bridesmaid or usher as it is a fun role without the same amount of pressure. Being a maid of honour or best man can be very stressful and hard work. Some people will be glad of the lesser role. Your wedding day is your day. So make sure divas and difficult people who are just going to upset you are not part of your wedding entourage. For the true friends in your life, honour them by giving them something important to do: a speech, being a witness or giving a reading.

If your female friend who you choose to honour is married then she is the matron of honour, if not she is the maid of honour or chief bridesmaid. Not many woman like being called 'matron' however so just ask for a preference.

The **Maid of Honour's** duty is to be the bride's wing woman. She is a sounding board, can be there when the dress is bought, keeps the other bridesmaids in line, helps out on the day. She is a therapist and a saint basically. She also plans the hen night. Will help the bride get into her wedding dress on the day and makes sure her makeup and hair look good all day. It can be quite the job and is not always fun. My maid of honour (who actually got engaged on the exact same day my fiancé and I did) was the best maid of honour EVER. She also made an amazing speech and I recommend all brides get their maid of honour to make a speech, otherwise all of the men get to have all of the fun and it is a little bit sexist. I have an interview with my amazing maid of honour, Paloma Kubiak, below.

How did it feel to be Maid of Honour?

I remember sitting in a Champagne and hot dog bar with Catherine having a catch-up and talking about the wedding which was set for the following summer. After lots of giggles and bubbles, I came home thinking Catherine may ask me to be her bridesmaid when we next meet up at a weird or wonderful location in London. But as she was slightly nervous, Catherine text me and asked whether I would be Maid of Honour. When I read the text, I was honoured, emotional and my obvious answer was 'yes'. I've been a bridesmaid twice; once for my cousin and once for one of my other best friends, so it was a real privilege to be the stand-out, right-hand lady for the bride. Catherine had already bought her dress but my only thought was to make her hen-do and Wedding Day extra special.

I wouldn't say being Maid of Honour was stressful – at times it was challenging as it seemed time was running out to plan the hen do and Catherine was trying to keep everyone happy above her own ideals of the wedding. I could tell at times she was stressed with it all and I tried to suggest the best ways to deal with conflicting family suggestions about flowers or seating arrangements etc. But on the day, it did all come together.

I'd say the hardest part about being Maid of Honour is knowing my place. Obviously I was Catherine's 'main gal' as the make-up/hairdresser put is so aptly, but I was also conscious that Catherine and James' family who I hadn't met before would also play a significant part in the day. It might sound silly but when Catherine's dress needed to be adjusted in the photos or her tiara needed to be pinned down so it wouldn't slip, I didn't know whether to dive in and do this or whether blood relatives would mind or want to do this themselves. Maybe it's just me being ultra self-conscious, but these thoughts did cross my mind. You'll be pleased to know that I did help out when not prompted by Catherine – I wanted her photos to be perfect and if that meant tucking in or adjusting clothing or the tiara, then it was my job to do this.

The easiest part about it all was that Catherine was the most undemanding bride ever. Previously I'd been chauffeur to visit wedding venues with my other friend, sampled wedding breakfasts, visited wedding fairs and been to textile altering shops many times with the bride. Catherine never once pouted if I couldn't make an event, fitting or run through. She seemed to have everything in control and so being Maid of Honour was a real pleasure.

How did you decide what to do for the hen night?

I've never had to organise a hen-do before and I really felt the pressure with this as I can't even seem to organise my own birthday or a catch-up with the girls!

The first thing I did was to get the email addresses of the girls Catherine wanted to celebrate with. The next thing was to pinpoint a date when we could all make it or at least the majority. The next thing I did was to write down all the things Catherine liked and was interested in. I knew for a fact it needed to be a classy, intimate and special occasion; Catherine wouldn't be smothered in 'L' plates or a stripper grinding on her lap.

Originally I had an idea of organising the hen do over the course of a weekend so the ladies could choose to attend any events that took their fancy and we could all spend a bit of time with the bride. So far we'd discussed clay-pigeon shooting, a casino and cocktail night, Champagne afternoon tea in London and even a trip to the cat café (Catherine's a real tea and cat person!). But budgets, transport and family commitments made these initial plans a little too complicated. Catherine shares a travel dream of mine – we both want to go to Las Vegas so I wanted to go back to basics and organise just one amazing night and bring Las Vegas to London. This was a real hit with the other hens and so I booked the Palm Beach Casino in Mayfair which offered a learn to play session so we'd be taught some of the tricks of the trade before hitting the decks with the big spenders. As it was such a special occasion, the Casino offered us a complementary glass of Champagne too which was a nice personal touch.

We also organised the Champagne tea at Catherine's flat in Putney. I had to ask James, the groom, to leave the flat for a few hours while we started celebrations there. James - ever the gent - naturally obliged. The original plan was for James to take Catherine out the flat for an hour, leaving the keys for me to find so I could decorate the flat. But as a journalist, Catherine was far too inquisitive and it just wasn't possible to get her out for that length of time on her hen do without her getting suspicious! So plan B, the not so glamorous option, was for Catherine to stay in her bedroom as I decorated the flat. Armed with cakes, bubbly, tea, confetti and sandwiches, the flat gave the Ritz a run for its money. The other hens started to arrive and we put the finishing touches in and when Catherine came out of her room, she was shocked and surprised. It was lovely to see her so touched and happy.

The theme was black tie glam and every single lady looked stunning. We did have a few silly things planned too for the night so it wasn't all too serious. We wrote

down truth or dares on paper then put them inside balloons to pop. Whatever fell out of your balloon, you'd have to do that night. Also, don't under-estimate the humour involved in 'pegging' people. In such a posh area, it was funny to witness men in their expensive suits walking around with a peg we'd manage to attach to them!

All in all, we all had an amazing, unforgettable night and it was nice to see the special ladies in her life surrounding the bride as she smiled despite losing all her casino chips!

How much planning was required?

I probably dedicated at least a couple of hours each week to plan the hen do over a three-month period. From asking friends for recommendations, to researching venues, ideas, checking food and drink menus, transport options and keeping in touch with all the hens via email. As James naturally wouldn't be there, I still wanted him to play a part in the hen do. I wanted to do a 'Mr and Mrs' style questionnaire where I'd ask James some questions and then Catherine had to guess what he answered. This took a bit of planning as I had to think of some great questions, and strike the right balance between sweet and funny. As with any event you organise, you want everyone to get on and have fun, so I was naturally nervous as some of the girls hadn't met before and I just wanted Catherine to have a good send off.

How was the wedding day?

I look back and I still can't believe how composed Catherine seemed on her wedding day which was full of emotion, anxiety and stress, more so than the average wedding jitters. After months of planning, nothing can prepare you for when your husband-to-be has spent the best part of the night before his wedding day in A&E and he wakes up to say 'I want to marry you but I don't know if I can'.

The Wedding Survival Guide

When Catherine text me from the hospital, at first I thought it was a joke but the seriousness of the situation soon became clear. It was a gorgeous, sunny day, perfect for the wedding and Catherine had told me to be round for 10am. But I approached the flat after midday as I didn't want to get in the way and thought the couple could both do with a few extra hours sleep. As I walked up the steps towards Catherine, I had no idea what to expect and when I saw her, she looked unusually calm. It was only in the last 30 minutes or so before the bridal party left that she was shaking uncontrollably.

The wedding itself was beautiful. I, along with a few others, couldn't help but get emotional. James was doing his best to get through the ceremony and have the strength to stand during the vows. Despite being so ill, everyone caught the tender glimpses and smiles between the couple – we could all tell they were very much in love. We also all knew that this would be unlike any other wedding as the bride and

groom may go off to hospital at any moment. But Mr and Mrs Yardley posed for photos with family and friends and even sat for the wedding breakfast. James, barely able to eat anything had to go for a lie down while everyone ate the three course, Italian inspired cuisine. Soon after, James and Catherine left to go back to the hospital and her parting words were for everyone to enjoy the rest of the evening. Without the couple, there were no twinkling stars, but everyone shuffled their feet on the dance floor, toasted each other for the health of James and watched as the sun slowly set across the Thames.

What are your top maid of honour tips?

One of my top tips for being Maid of Honour is to be decisive – set a date, time and venue and stick with it. While choice can be good and provide flexibility to accommodate people, at other times it's more of a problem as they can't make up their minds or may take time to get back to you. By telling guests exactly when and where you want them, you're in control, something you need to have as the bride's right hand woman.

Saying that, don't be afraid to ask others for help. I may have known Catherine for six years but I've never worked with her on the stage or in photo shoots, so different people may be able to provide different ideas about what the bride would like to do on her hen do, for instance.

Being Maid of Honour isn't just about helping the bride pick her dress or choose the flowers for the big day. You do have a little extra responsibility and some of that is simply being there when she needs to chat and knowing when to say the right things. I'm a rubbish liar, but on the wedding day when Catherine was panicking about being late as she thought of James standing the altar in so much pain, I had to tell her that everything was going to be okay. The wedding would still go ahead; it's the bride's prerogative to be late, though I was conscious that we needed to get to the venue as soon as possible so James didn't have to suffer in-front of the awaiting guests.

My other tip is to always have a 'plan B'. When it became apparent that the hen do weekend wasn't possible, I had to think on my feet and come up with alternative plans.

Would you do it again?

I would definitely plan the hen do again and I'd love to be Maid of Honour again for Catherine. Despite the panic of changing plans and venues and at first not being able to co-ordinate all the ladies and the fact that James was so ill, they did get married and it was a remarkable day. It was a pleasure witnessing Catherine

become Mrs Yardley and we all have wonderful memories from both the hen do and the actual wedding day itself.

Thank you Paloma.

Best Man. The best man does everything the maid of honour does, only for the groom. He buys the outfit with the groom, is his wingman and arranges the stag do.

Bridesmaids. Look pretty, walk down the aisle with the bride. They are basically maids for the bride but in a girlfriend kind of way rather than a servant kind of way. My bridesmaids were Paloma, my friend Holly, cousin-in-law Flora and sister-in-law Alexandra. They were all amazing and looked gorgeous on the day.

Flower girl: an adorable young child who is old enough to walk to the end of the aisle by herself, throwing petals along the way.

Ushers. Like maids to the groom and the wedding in general. Ushers keep a wedding running smoothly but you don't need to have them. We didn't have any. If you have a small wedding they will probably not be needed. Ushers help guests know where they are going to sit, give directions to the other venue or anywhere else that is needed. One usher per fifty guests is the general rule. Like all members of the bridal party they are ambassadors for the bride and groom. There to be courteous, polite and endlessly helpful. Make sure you get them all a little gift afterwards. Or a big one.

OTHER THINGS TO CONSIDER

Research

There is a wealth of information out there. More than ever as there is now an explosion of wedding blogs and Pinterest has wedding ideas and pictures galore. Wedding magazines are always fun and full of advice and beautiful pictures. They are quite expensive however. hitched.com is an incredibly helpful resource. I found my wedding venue through them. My online magazine http://frostmagazine.com also has some wedding inspiration.

Pinterest

Pinterest is a godsend for brides. If you don't know what it is already; it is basically a virtual scrapbook. You can 'pin' different images from the internet onto different boards, putting together a virtual collage. You can also look at other people's boards. There are plenty of wedding ones.

Insurance

Weddings are hugely expensive and if you add up all of the deposits you might start crying. If the deposit money really does start to add up you might want to take out

some wedding insurance. This will cover you against illness, venue problems and weather issues.

Loans

I do not recommend taking out a loan to pay for your wedding. It is not worth starting your married life in debt.

Online Shopping

A lot of online shopping sites can help when it comes to wedmin. *Not On The High Street* have a lot of great stuff which could be used for favours or gifts for the wedding party. They also do lots of great wedding stuff. EBay and Amazon are also your friends. They also have quite good refund policies in place.

Bargain Hunting.

H&M have great dresses from just £59.99 and Minna have sustainable bespoke dresses at an affordable price. Wilkinson have things like chalkboards for under £5 that can be used for decoration. IKEA and H&M are also good for furniture which you can reuse after the wedding. You can also reuse things you have around the house or that friends might have. An old suitcase is a cute addition to put cards in. Car boot sales and charity shops will also have some great stuff.

Inspiration

Bridal magazines and blogs are a good bet. Brides Magazine is a good one, as is Wedding, You and Your Wedding, Perfect Wedding and Elle magazine has now launched a wedding magazine. All of the main women's magazines tend to have wedding sections on their website. Such as Marie Claire, Grazia and Elle. Others tend to have some good wedding articles.

Here is a rather amazing site which lists the Top 100 Wedding Blogs: http://www.weddingblogs100.com I had a lot of fun on this site in the run up to my wedding. There are some truly great sites there. You can also check out the wedding section of my online magazine, Frost Magazine: http://www.frostmagazine.com/category/weddings-2/

Rock N Roll Bride was the first-ever UK based wedding blog and is now hugely popular. It is a great site, especially if you want an alternative wedding or just something a little bit different. There are also great real-life weddings on the site with amazing pictures. Great for inspiration.

A great idea for putting together the scrapbook of your wedding together is Pinterest. If you have not heard of Pinterest, it is a site on which you can 'pin' pictures from other sites to specific boards. You just register and then you can start pinning straight away. It is lots of fun and makes things easier. Register here: http://www.pinterest.com and they also have lots of wedding stuff already there: http://www.pinterest.com/all/weddings/

Pick a date.

After you pick a date you can get on with everything else. If you pick a date during peak wedding season then keep in mind that you will have to book some of your suppliers well in advance, especially if you are getting married on a weekend. If you are getting married on a weekday there will be less pressure, although Fridays can also get booked up quite far in advance.

YOUR DREAM WEDDING: WANTS AND COMPROMISES.

You may have a specific idea of your wedding in mind but the reality will probably be different. This doesn't need to be a bad thing. Just choose the things that you are not willing to negotiate on. When you know what is most important and worth spending money on you can focus on that and then look at cheaper options for other things. Or rope family and friends in. Most will be happy to help.

Budget.

This is the tough one but you need to work out what it is and then you need to stick to it. Enquire if any family members can help and then sit down with your fiancé and have a proper discussion about what you can and cannot afford. There is no point in going into debt for a wedding or taking out a loan. It is only one day of your life, an important one, but one day. You can have an amazing wedding on a small bud get. No one should start their married life in debt. Watch out for the 'W' bomb. As in 'wedding'. The w word makes everyone vastly put their prices up.

Guessing cost.

Always overestimate. That way you won't be left short. Always remember VAT. Some venues and suppliers will be coy about whether VAT is included but ask them and get a direct answer and then make a note of it.

How much it will cost.

This is the question. The answer is: quite a bit. My husband and I managed to get married for less than £10,000. We paid for the majority of this ourselves but did have some family members contribute. Not bad when the average wedding costs £21,000. Spreadsheets are your friend. Negotiating will also be your friend. Try to get money off everything. Don't take the first quote and rope family and friends into the planning if money is tight.

Controlling Costs.

This is very important. Watch out for VAT and always account for everything. Use a spreadsheet if you can. Keep an eye on the small things as they can all add up.

Dealing With Suppliers.

When dealing with suppliers always remember that you are the customer. Be polite but always be firm. Read the small print and make your wishes clear. More importantly, don't pay any final invoices until everything has been checked. One supplier charged us for VAT despite the fact they said they wouldn't. Hmm. Always be careful.

Hatton Gardens. Hatton Gardens is the area in London where all of the jewellers are located. You can get a very good deal here.

Spreadsheets

Spreadsheets are your friend. If you don't know how to do one then quickly brush up your skills. They will be your saving grace. Have one for your wedding budget and one for your wedding guest list. For the wedding guest list one, leave space for information such as dietary requirements, RSVP received, gift given and thank you card sent.

Organisation Tips

Have everyone's contact details to hand. Use spreadsheets and have plenty 'to do' lists. Make sure your partner pulls his or her weight. Weddings are hard and stressful to organise, don't go it alone.

Wedding Planner: To Go It Alone Or Hire Help.

If I had the money I would have hired a wedding planner in an instant. However, they are expensive and you don't really need one. I am not saying that in a rude way, they will save time and probably a lot of money but weighing up the cost is important. Your venue might have a wedding planner or venue coordinator onsite. If so, this is a tremendous bonus.

If you get a wedding planner make sure you check their recommendations and also have a clear idea of what you want. It is their job to take your ideas and make them into the wedding of your dreams. Don't accept anything less, budget permitting.

Order of Service.

You do not need an order of service. Religious ceremonies typically have one. The order of service should have your wedding details on the front.

Order of Service

The Wedding of Sarah Jones and Paul Woodward

14th of July 2014

St Joseph's Church, London

You would then have the music, hymns and readings inside, along with any other details and the order of service. You could include any prayers and the details of the wedding party along with any thanks.

You may want to give one to your band/DJ and other suppliers.

Rehearsal

Rehearsals are not really done in the United Kingdom. If you really want one, you could ask the venue whether it is possible although they may charge you.

Run-throughs

Ditto.

CHAPTER 2: THE CEREMONY.

CEREMONY

Where you can get married will change according to your religion. Find your religion below to find churches in your area if you are having a religious ceremony. If you are having a civil ceremony then contact your local council. You will have to register to give notice there anyway. They should have a list of venues.

Baptist Union baptist.org.uk
British Humanist Association humanism.org.uk
Catholic Church catholichurch.org.uk
Catholic Marriage Care marriage care.org.uk
Church of England churchofengland.org.uk
Church of England Faculty Office faculatyoffice.org.uk
Church of Scotland churchofscotland.org.uk
General Register Office for England and Wales direct.gov.uk
General Register Office for Scotland geo-scotland.gov.uk
Greek Orthodox Archdiocese thyateira.org.uk
Humanist Society of Scotland humanism-scotland.org.uk
Jewish Marriage Council jmc-uk.org
The Methodist Church methodist.org.uk
The United Reformed Church urc.org.uk

Faith Weddings

For the religious.

Civil Ceremony

For the non-religious who just want to get legally married. You cannot have anything religious in a civil ceremony.

Readings

You can choose anything you want. A passage from a book, poems, even song lyrics. There are plenty of resources to give you inspiration online.

CEREMONY MUSIC.

The ceremony will need music. If you are getting married in a church you can play religious music but if you are having a civil ceremony nothing religious is allowed. You could have a choir, a soloist or maybe the church will have an organist. Musicians playing the violin or something similar is a nice touch. We had our Uncle Matthew playing the lute at our wedding. He was brilliant and the guests loved it.

You could have an MP3 player or an iPod. Even a CD will do. Just make sure you have someone cueing the music and that they know the right song to play at the right moment. If you are using an iPod then make sure you have a playlist called 'ceremony'. This will make it easier for those who have to work it.

Here are Some Song Choices…

For the brides' entrance:

Civil

Morning Mood - E.Greig
Intermezzo - Mascagni
Wedding March - Felix Mendelssohn
Air on the G String - J.S Bach
Love Me Tender - Elvis Presley
Beautiful Day - U2
Baby It's You - The Beatles

Religious

The Prince of Denmark - J.Clarke
Gloria in excelsis Deo - A. Vivaldi
Trumpet Tune in D - H.Purcell
Dance of the Blessed Spirits - Gluck
Barcarolle - Offenbach
If ye Love Me - T. Tallis
Arrival of The Queen of Sheba - Handel

Signing of the Register.

Civil

What a Wonderful World - Louis Armstrong
Feeling Good - Nina Simone
Chanson de Matin - E.Elgar
One Love - U2
All of Me - John Legend

Religious

Ave Maria - F. Schubert
The Lord bless you and keep you - J.Rutter
Ave Verum Corpus - Mozart
Melody in F - Rubinstein
To a Wild Rose - MacDowell

Bride And Groom Exit

Civil

Walking On Sunshine - Katrina and The Waves
Can't Help Falling in Love - Elvis Presley
When I Fall in Love - Nat King Cole
At Last - Etta James
Signed, Sealed, Delivered I'm Yours - Stevie Wonder

Religious

Hallelujah Chorus - G.F Handel
Toccata From Symphony No. 5 - C.M. Widor
La Réjouissance - G.F Handel
Trumpet Tune - Purcell
Wedding March   Wagner

Religious Hymns.

Amazing Grace
All Things Bright And Beautiful
Praise Ye The Lord
The Lord's My Shepherd
Morning Has Broken
Jerusalem
Glorious Things of Thee Are Spoken
Dear Lord and Father of Mankind
Come to a Wedding

GIVING NOTICE.

Making It Legal.

A marriage is a legal contract and as such it is subject to some legal requirements. The first one being that you must give notice or banns.

You need a marriage licence to get married. (In Scotland and Northern Ireland referred to as a 'marriage schedule'). This authorises you to get married and then after you get married you will have a marriage certificate that proves that you are.

When you do get your marriage certificate you should order some extra copies. If you order them before the wedding they are usually cheaper. You have to mail an original copy of your marriage certificate if you change your name and apply for a new national insurance card or driving licence. You will worry less if you have a few extra copies.

To get married both you and your future spouse must be:

At least 16-years-old to get married, or a same sex couple if you want to register a civil partnership. You will need parental consent in England, Northern Ireland and Wales if you are under 18.

You must be 'free to marry' which means you should both be single, widowed or divorced, or in a civil partnership which has since been dissolved.

You will have to give notice to marry and then after sixteen days you can marry. Sometimes the sixteen days varies depending on location, but it is typically about a fortnight.

You have two options when you marry: civil or religious ceremony.

A civil ceremony is a legally approved marriage which hasn't, and isn't allowed, any religious parts. You can have a civil ceremony in any register office or at any venue that is licensed to hold wedding ceremonies. Booking a register office is the cheaper option but you will still need to hold your reception somewhere else. The easier option is to have your ceremony and reception in the one place. This also helps with transport and avoids any traffic issues. You will have to pay the registrar an extra fee to go to the venue.

Enfield Register Office charges the following as of 1 July 2014.

Marriage Certificates: £4 each - on day of registration only

- Notice fee £35 per person
- Mon - Wed Simple Ceremony in the Admiral's Suite £120
- Friday Enhanced Ceremony in the Admiral's Suite £200
- Saturday Enhanced Ceremony in the Admiral's Suite £300
- Mon - Sun at an approved premise £450
- Mon - Sun at an approved premise after 6pm £650
- Certificates - on day of registration only £4 each
- Certificates thereafter £10 each

Wandsworth Register Office charge the following.

Weekday wedding at Wandsworth Register Office £45
Victoria Room: weekday £100 weekend £130
Alexandra Room: weekday £150 Saturday £220
Approved venues in Wandsworth: weekday £280 Saturday £350 Sunday £380
Marriage certificates cost £4 each.

Marriage fees in **America** range from $10 to $115, depending on which state you marry in.

These are the prices to get married in **Scotland**:

For each person submitting a notice of marriage, civil or religious, to the district registrar £30

For solemnisation of a civil marriage £55. For each extract of the entry in the register of marriages (applied for within one month of registration of the marriage, civil or religious) £10.

Two people could thus give notice of marriage, have a civil marriage solemnised by the registrar in a registration office, and have one extract of the register entry (their 'marriage certificate') for the total in statutory fees of £125

For more information on marrying in Scotland go to http://www.gro-scotland.gov.uk/regscot/getting-married-in-scotland/i-want-to-get-married-in-scotland-how-do-i-go-about-it.html"

If one of you is living abroad it may be possible to give notice of your intention to marry in the country in which you live, as long as that country has signed up to the British Subjects Facilities Act. You can visit www.gov.uk/marriages-civil-partnerships for information that is up-to-date.

Civil Ceremony

Civil ceremonies are the most popular type of wedding in the UK, accounting for seventy per cent of all marriages. To book a civil ceremony you need to call up your local register office and give notice to marry. This costs £35 each. Yes, already adding up isn't it? You must do this with your local register office even if you do not intend to get married in your local area. You can do this up to a year before your wedding but you must do it 15 days before. This is the same for heterosexual and homosexual marriages.

You will have to attend the giving notice appointment with your fiancé and will also have to bring along proof of identity and proof of address. These could be your passport and a bill. The registrar will tell you what to bring and make sure that you do because if you don't you will have to do the entire thing again. If either of you is divorced then you will have to bring your decree absolute. If either of you is widowed you will need to bring the marriage and death certificate. You and your fiancé will be interviewed separately but it is nothing to worry about. You will just be asked a few questions. After the appointment a certificate of marriage will be issued and you can marry after sixteen days. You will need two people to sign the marriage register and act as witnesses. It will help to let them know they are doing this as we forgot to inform our witnesses so no one came forward when the registrar asked them to.

After you have given notice the papers will be posted within the registry office for public view. If anyone wants to oppose the marriage they have fifteen days to do so. If no one objects, and why would they? you can collect the marriage licence after fifteen days if you are marrying outside of your district. Otherwise the registrar will take it to the venue.

Your certificate will only be valid for twelve months and only for your chosen venue. If you change your venue or don't get married within the year then you need to register again.

For a civil ceremony you have to marry in a licensed venue or a register office. The venue has to be open to the public and the doors cannot be locked. The venue also has to be a permanent structure. If you have any doubts contact your local authority. You have to have lived in the district you are giving notice in for at least seven days. This can be a hotel if you are based abroad. If the venue of your choice is not in your district you still have to register in your district first and then you can contact the register office where you want to get married or your venue is based.

A civil ceremony generally takes about ten to fifteen minutes. This will depend on the vows you choose and whether or not you have asked a guest to come up and do a wedding reading or a song. In a civil ceremony you can include readings, music and a song but nothing religious.

The registrar will make a short statement about marriage and then go into your vows. When you get the leaflet that has all of the vows on it can be intimidating but don't worry, even if you choose them all the ceremony would not be that long. Just go through them and tick the ones you want or even write your own. Some of the vows cannot be changed as these are the part of the ceremony that is legally binding and a verbal contract.

Religious Ceremony.

For a faith wedding you can get married in a church, chapel or registered religious building. Even if you want to get married in a religious ceremony you may have to register your marriage at your register office.

If you are having an Anglican or a Church of England wedding then you don't usually have to register at a register office. The officials who perform the marriage will give notice and register the marriage.

Preparation for a religious ceremony will change depending on what your religion is. To be extra safe, talk to your religious officiant to make sure you have covered everything before your wedding. Generally for a religious ceremony, instead of giving notice, banns (a formal announcement of the proposed marriage) will be read in the church of each partner and in the church where the marriage will take place if it is different on three Sundays before the ceremony takes place.

For some Christian religious ceremonies you will still need a registrar to make it legal and provide a marriage certificate so double check with your officiant. You

could also check with your local register office as they will know whether or not the venue where you want to get married is registered to do weddings.

Some religious weddings will require you to give notice at the register office at least sixteen days before the wedding. Not all ministers and priests are authorised to give notice or register your marriage.

Church of England and Anglican Weddings.

The wedding must take place in a recognised religious building. The doors must be unlocked and the wedding must take place between 8am and 6pm. The ceremony can take place on any day of the week as long as the minster, vicar or reverend agrees. Getting a Sunday might be hard however.

When you meet the minister you will have to take the following:

Your baptism certificate.
Passport and/or birth certificate.
Written parental consent if you are under eighteen.
Decree absolutes if divorced or death certificate if widowed.

The minister will read out the banns on three consecutive Sundays within three months before the wedding date. The banns declare the couple's intention to marry and give people a chance to object. If you are not marrying in your usual church then the banns will have to be read there as well. Check your parish boundaries to make sure all is correct, they may not follow modern postcode boundaries. The minister will issue and sign the marriage certificate after the ceremony.

For full details check out the Church of England website at www.yourchurchwedding.org

Catholic Wedding.

The below also applies to Russian and Greek weddings.

You must give notice if you are having a civil wedding in a catholic church if the Catholic church is listed as the venue of marriage. A civil registrar may need to attend in some situations, not to conduct the ceremony however, but to arrange the signing of the register and handle the paperwork. An appointed person from the church may be allowed. Things can vary greatly so you should check early. Especially as the day you want to get married may get booked up.

Jewish Wedding.

Jewish weddings are not subject to the same licensing restrictions as civil weddings. They can take place in a synagogue. They also do not have to take place in a permanent structure so you could get married outside.

If you are being married by a rabbi then you give notice at your local register office as you would for a civil ceremony. You then pass the notices on to the rabbi. A civil registrar will have to attend in some situations to sign the paperwork. In most cases the rabbi will bring an appointed person to officiate the ceremony or sign the certificate.

Marrying Abroad.

A destination wedding is generally done over a long weekend. These can be hard but if you have your heart set on it then you can have a memorable and wonderful time, along with your guests.

There are a number of reasons why a destination wedding might work for you and your spouse-to-be:

Families are far apart and the location is in a neutral and fair place.
The country has a special meaning for the couple.
To keep the wedding intimate, with only close friends and family.
To save money. Fewer guests mean less money and some destinations are much cheaper.
To make the wedding exotic.

Destination weddings will cost a lot in flights, accommodation and travel. Only the people who really love you will spend money on airfare and hotels if you are marrying somewhere where travel costs are expensive. There is always the option of paying for your guests' flight but not many people can afford this. So keep this in mind. On the bright side, fewer people means less money you need to spend on guests. Another good idea if you are worried about the cost to guests is to have the wedding in Europe. It is much cheaper to get there than America or Australia.

If you do have a wedding abroad then your guests will have spent a lot of money to get there and attend. You must treat them as guests and look after them well. Maybe you could arrange some activities and inviting them to a pre-wedding dinner would also be a wonderful gesture. Make sure you arrange transportations for your guests. A lovely favour, which doesn't have to be horrendously expensive would also be appreciated. Also make sure that you give your guest all of the information they will need on travel and booking hotels, along with contact names and details of any vital people. Include what the weather will be like, the dress code and any travel requirements. A run-down of what exactly will be happening is also a good idea. You should be able to get a discount if you have a large group booking. You might also want to include child-care information if your guests have children and you are inviting children to your wedding.

The Wedding Survival Guide

When you send out your save-the-date cards or invites it would be a good idea to send an email or a letter within with the following information in detail: why you chose that location, flight information, accommodation information, information on transportation, activities, weather, childcare, dress code and where you and your future spouse can be contacted if people have any questions.

What usually happened with overseas weddings is that the guests are responsible for their own flights and accommodation and then you pay for all of the events that happen over the weekend.

Go to a destination off-peak, ask the travel agent for a discount for group bookings and always check the weather. A travel agent will have essential knowledge of whether or not the location and the timing of going there is a good idea or not. Negotiate heavily with the hotel, try to get a room upgrade for yourself and try and to get perks like welcome baskets or free lunch included. Also be aware that you might be financially responsible for hotel rooms even if some of your guests don't turn up. A nice welcome note and even a goody bag with maps and cute little things inside provided by you will be much appreciated by your guests. Especially after they have made such an effort to get there.

If you get married in a truly beautiful location then you won't have to worry about dressing the venue.

Below are the top destinations for weddings abroad.

America.
Australia.
Austria.
Bermuda.
Canada.
The Caribbean.
Cyprus.
France
Greece.
Iceland.
Italy.
Seychelles.
South Africa.
Spain.
Thailand.

Your marriage should be recognised by UK law as long as it fulfils the legal requirements on age and being free to marry. Your saving grace will be The Foreign Office website which has a lot of information and will also direct you to the British Embassy in the country you want to marry. You should check with a lawyer and the local authorities in the location where you want to get married to be safe.

Getting married abroad will not be easy. In fact it is notoriously hard and if you do not know the local language it will be even more so. If you can afford a wedding planner with a good reputation in the local area, then go for it. Otherwise think carefully and make sure it is worth it. You will drown in bureaucracy and administration. However, if it is your dream and you have a high tolerance for stress, go for it.

Many couples get around this by having their legal ceremony in the UK and then having a reception abroad. It is important to make sure that your marriage is legal in the country you marry and your native country too. This is a very good idea and you could even have a blessing/fake ceremony abroad. Just make sure it is all legal as legal requirements will change from country to country. If you don't you may find out further down the line that you are not actually married like Mike Jagger and Jerry Hall did. Their wedding in Bali ended up being annulled.

Another idea to keep costs down is to have everything done in-house. Getting an all-inclusive deal will save stress, time and money. Embracing the local culture will also save money. Getting your flowers locally instead of importing English roses will save a fortune.

A number of travel agencies have designated wedding departments to help you with your overseas wedding. Having an expert to hand is always a brilliant idea and they could actually save you money. They will help you with the paperwork and can recommend suppliers. They might also offer wedding packages. Check what these packages include and watch out for any extra charges. Some packages will include flights, registrar, accommodation, cake, food, a bouquet and a photographer. The actual wedding planning will probably be done by the venue manager when you arrive.

Travel agencies which have wedding departments include Thomson (www.thomson.co.uk), Sandals (www.sandals.com), First Choice (www.firstchoice.com), Kuoni (www.kuoni.com) and Virgin Holidays (www.virginholidays.com).

Check with your registrar or minister that there haven't been any law changes since this book was published. Contacting the tourist board of the location you want to marry in will also give you invaluable information. The British Embassy in the country you are marrying in will also be very helpful. They will be able to make sure you have all of the documents you need.

Most countries will need the following three months before the wedding:

A valid ten-year passport.
Birth certificate.
Your decree absolute if you are divorced.
An affidavit signed by your solicitor which states that there are no legal objections against your marriage.

Your adoption certificate if you are adopted.

If you have been widowed you will need the death certificate and marriage certificate of your former spouse.

You can obtain a Certificate of No Impediment (CNI) from your local British Consulate or Embassy. The venue or the travel agent may ask for one. Check whether you need a CNI in the country you are getting married in. More information here: www.gov.uk/government/publications/certificate-of-no-impediment-and-nulla-ostas

Hiring a wedding planner either in the UK or the country you are getting married in is a good idea if you can afford it. It may even save you money. If you hire one in the UK then make sure they specialise in the area you want to get married in. You don't want to be a guinea pig, your wedding is far too important for that.

If you are having your wedding abroad the best thing to do is combine your wedding and honeymoon. This will save money and be the logical thing to do. You could also have a proper honeymoon-wedding: this would be just you and your fiancé getting married with two witnesses and then having your honeymoon afterwards. This can be very intimate and some places will also include the add-on wedding either cheaply or for free.

Overseas Wedding Checklist.

Will you and your guests require vaccinations?
What documents are needed to legally marry?
Is it hurricane or tornado season? What is the weather going to be like on your wedding day?
Do any documents have to be sent before the wedding?
Will the travel and accommodation be affordable to guests?
Will you need witnesses?
What are the religious and legal requirements to get married in your chosen destination?
Are there any residential requirements?
How difficult is it to get to the destination?
Will you need proof of divorce or proof of being widowed?
Will you need any blood tests or immunisations to be granted a marriage license?
Is it easy to get any supplies you might need in the area?
Do you speak the local language?
Will any of your documents need to be translated into the native language?
Are original documents needed?
How long will it take to get your marriage licence?
Can you visit the venue/location beforehand?
How long before the wedding should you arrive?

So if you want to have your wedding abroad it is possible, just be prepared for lots of bureaucracy, administration and stress. Also take into account time differences.

You may have to contact people at midnight your time and check if you can talk via Skype to save your phone bill. It is also visual so you can see the person and also any flowers etc. that you are planning for your wedding. Also enquire whether or not people speak English. You may need an interpreter.

Some countries will require that you live there for a certain period of time before you can get married.

The following countries do not require a period of residency but make sure that you do not need to meet the registrar before the wedding: Australia, Austria, Antigua, Barbados, Bermuda, Croatia, Gibraltar, Italy, Malta, New Zealand, Portugal, Spain, St Lucia, South Africa, Turkey, Thailand and some states in the United States. New York requires a twenty-four hour stay.

These countries require between one day to a week: Anguilla, British Virgin Islands, Bahamas, Cook Islands, Greece, Cyprus, Dominican Republic, Grenada, Jamaica, Mexico, Mauritius, Sri Lanka and the Seychelles.

Bali requires ten days and France requires forty continuous days.

All above correct at time of going to press.

Make sure you inform your bank and your credit card company that you are going away. Otherwise they may cancel your cards when they see a lot of money going out in a foreign location.

You may also want to think of your style of wedding dress carefully. You will expand in the heat. I got married in July on one of the hottest days of the year and the dress that was just slightly loose three days before fitted perfectly. Thank god for the last-minute stress-induced weight loss!

Packing for a holiday is stressful at the best of times but this is compounded when packing for your wedding. Especially when forgetting something can ruin the entire thing. No pressure! Here is a helpful checklist of things to pack.

Wedding dress. Quite important.
Wedding Shoes plus other accessories like underwear, jewellery, veil and tiara.
The groom's outfit and shoes. Don't forget ties, cravats or cufflinks.
The rings.
Stationery like place cards and order of service.
All of your important paperwork. Include all of your emails with the venue and travel agent or anyone else involved in the wedding.
Wedding makeup. It might be hard to find the lipstick you have your heart set on elsewhere.
An iPod filled with your wedding music. Can be used as a backup or instead of a band/DJ.
Gifts for the wedding party if you are not buying them when you get there.

The Wedding Survival Guide

A first aid kit would be a very good idea. Include insect repellent, SPF, aftersun, antihistamines, paracetamol, plasters and anything else you can think of.
Other essentials will include a sewing kit, perfume, baby wipes, body tape, hairspray, deodorant, a lint remover, mints, flat shoes, shoe polish, sanitary towels, a piece of white chalk to cover up smudges on your dress, clear nail varnish for runs on tights or stockings, nail file, hair brush and hair clips, tissues, toothbrush and toothpaste.

If the wedding you are having abroad is small then you could also have a lavish celebration when you return to the UK. You could even theme it to the location of your wedding. There will also be less sour grapes from people who could not attend.

CHAPTER 3: OTHER LEGAL STUFF

Prenups.

Pre-nuptial agreements didn't have much power in the United Kingdom until recently. They are slowly being taken more seriously. Unlike in the United States where prenups are legally binding. In fact, if a couple gets married in California, and then divorces, their assets get split 50/50.

Deciding Whether To Change Your Name.

It is entirely up to you whether or not you change your name. Many women don't and sometimes men do. Some older relatives and in-laws might pressure you or might make a dig but just be firm and polite with them and make sure your husband has a gentle word with them if it gets too much.

Many newspapers and magazines may still make comments when a woman doesn't change her surname to her new husband's and Tatler may still call the women in the Bystander section solely by their husbands name (!) but it helps to ignore such stupid sexism.

A woman's surname does not automatically change just because she marries. Nor do you have to legally change it. In fact, an estimated 36 per cent of woman now keep their maiden name after they marry.

This was my wedding diary entry on women changing their names after marriage.

We live in modern times and tradition is something ever-changing. Some traditional things last, and some just don't. Others, like a woman taking her husband's name after they marry, actually become controversial. My favourite motto to live by in life is, 'live and let live'. But, yet, it seems we can't.

Some women see submission or sexism when a woman changes her name. But where did that woman get her name? And where did her mother get hers?, and her grandmother? To stop it now feels like closing the stable after the horse has long bolted.

All of this does make me sound pro changing my name, I know. I am in a bit of a muddle with it to be honest. Part of my thinks it is something to do if you have children, so you can be a family unit, the stories of women being stopped at airports because they have a different surname from their children are common. If I have children I certainly don't want to have a different surname from them. It would just be too weird. This means I have to take my fiancé's name, he has to take mine or we have to double-barrel our names. That is if we have children. If we don't, does it really matter? Part of me thinks not.

There is a part in The Crucible when John Proctor has two choices: change his name or die. He chooses to die, 'It is my name,' he says, 'I cannot have any other'. This is a pretty extreme example but I remember watching TV with a friend. There was a woman with a double-barreled surname. My friend commented on the ridiculousness of her name; "Oh, just lose your ego woman!" But it is not just ego is it? It's your identity. My name is me. Well, actually, my name is a stage name, albeit one that I use for everything now. It belonged to my grandmother, a British-Lithuanian who died when she was only 40 of kidney failure. Not surprisingly, I would like this to live on. I am only a handful of people in the world with the surname 'Balavage'. An Anglo take on 'Bullovich'. You see? Surnames, they change. As does identity. I even pronounce my surname differently than she would have: Ba-Lav-age, with a quiet 'V'. At my friends Nick Cohen's book launch, the amazing writer Francis Wheen complimented my on my surname, 'Like a glamorous French actress'. I have pronounced it the way he said it ever since.

So when I marry I have a few choices: change my real name and keep my stage name, change my name completely and just keep Balavage for acting, or double-barrel my name. I have until next year to decide, but I am already in a pickle. What to do?

It is not about feminism or inequality. If a woman wants to take her new husband's name, she should be able to, if a man wants to change his, he should and if a woman wants to keep or double-barrel her name, she should be able to without rudeness: it's her identity after all: Live and let live.

Options On What To Do With Your Name After You Marry.

The bride takes the groom's name.
The couple double-barrel their names.
The bride double-barrels her name.
The bride keeps her maiden name
The groom takes the bride's name.
The bride takes her husband's names but keeps her own surname for professional purposes.
The bride and groom meld their names together.
The bride and groom take on an entirely new name.

If you do change your name do consider that it might have consequences for your career. By the time many people get married they have usually built up their career in their chosen industry. Whilst I changed my legal name to my husband's surname it would have been career suicide to change my stage name this late in my life. I am not saying it would not have been possible but I have built up a name as a writer and actor and that wasn't something I was going to throw away just because I got married.

Another thing to keep in mind is that if your new spouse has debt then you might want to wait until it is paid off until you change your name. Otherwise you might get debt collectors harassing you.

CHANGING YOUR NAME.

If you do decide to change your name, whether male or female, here is how to do it.

Who To Notify And What To Do.

It is tedious and expensive but you will have to notify the following people. All identification and accounts will have to be changed.

HMRC.

You will have to notify HM Revenue & Customs. They will then automatically update all your details for tax and benefits. This includes national insurance, child benefit and self-assessment or pay-as-you-earn.

Passport.

Unfortunately you will need to pay for a new passport. Very annoying. You can apply for a new passport with your new surname three months before you get married in case you are jetting off straight away. Your old passport will be cancelled during this time. Your new passport will also be postdated so you will not be able to use it before the ceremony.

You can get a form from your local Post Office, by requesting one from https://www.gov.uk/renew-adult-passport or applying online. At time of going to press it costs £72.50, or £81.25 through the Post Office's Passport Check and Send service. Time left on an existing passport is added to your new one - up to a maximum of 9 months. Which is a bit annoying if your passport has a lot of time left on it. It should take about three weeks to get your new passport.

Remember to book your holiday in the name of your new passport, or your old one if you are not changing your name until after. The name on your passport should match the name on your ticket. I had a bad experience after a friend booked a ticket but accidentally did it in my stage name. Ryanair charged me £100 to change it. Ouch.

Driving Licence.

To change your licence you will have to get a form from the Post Office

This is what the DVLA say about renewing your licence due to a name change:

Applying at a Post Office

A list of the closest Post Offices where you can renew your driving licence will be on the renewal form (D798) you receive in the post.

You can also find your nearest suitable Post Office on the Post Office website or you can call them.

The Post Office
Telephone: 0345 722 3344

You can't apply via the Post Office if your name has changed.

You need to take:

The Wedding Survival Guide

- ○ the completed renewal form D798
- ○ your photocard licence and paper counterpart if you have them
- ○ the fee of £20

The Post Office will charge an extra £4.50 fee to process your application.

Your driving licence should arrive within 3 weeks. It might take longer if your medical or personal details need to be checked.

You can't download a copy of form D798, but if you don't get your renewal reminder you may still be able to renew your licence at selected Post Offices. You need to have the photocard and paper counterpart of your current licence.

Applying by post

You need to fill in the licence renewal form D798 and include:

- ○ a new passport type photo taken within the last month (don't sign the back of the photo)
- ○ the photocard and paper counterpart of your current licence (you need to tick the relevant box on the D798 form if you've lost either part)
- ○ a cheque or postal order for £20, payable to DVLA (no fee is needed if you have a medical short period licence or you're aged 70 or over)

You also need to include identity documents if you've changed your name.

Send the application to:

DVLA
Swansea
SA99 1DH

If you don't have the reminder form.

If you don't have the D798 reminder and want to apply by post, fill in form D1 'Application for a driving licence', available from the DVLA form ordering service and selected Post Offices.

Your driving licence should arrive within 3 weeks. It might take longer if your medical or personal details need to be checked.

More information and the option to request a form here: https://www.gov.uk/renew-driving-licence#other-ways-to-apply

Other Records To Update.

Bank accounts. Don't forget a new cheque book.
Credit cards.
Insurance policies.
Retirement accounts.

Work records

Business cards (if applicable)
Electoral roll.
Email address.
Stationery.
Frequent flyer programmes.

Phew. Quite a task and very tedious. Most companies will let you change your name over the phone or by email. Banks will want a written request however and possibly even a copy of your marriage certificate.

If you are doing anything official it might help to carry your marriage certificate with you until you have your new passport and/or driving licence.

Deciding Not To Go Through With It.

Breaking off an engagement is an awful thing to have to go through and many people will be disappointed. However it is much better than going through a nasty divorce or marrying someone that you don't actually love. Don't be scared to call off an engagement if it is the right thing to do. It will cause less pain and heartache than going through with it, even if you lose some deposit money.

The first thing to do is to notify the venue, caterer and any other wedding suppliers that you have hired. Attempt to get all or most of your deposit back. If suppliers give a firm 'no' then you can dispute it via your credit card if you paid that way or you can contact the Citizens Advice Bureau.

If you took out wedding insurance, and you are covered for cold feet, then you are laughing.

In regards to guests: you must return their gifts to them.

If things with your now ex start to get messy, seek legal help.

You will have to return the engagement ring. There is some debate to this, legal and otherwise. Also, many feel that if the man broke off the engagement then the woman should be able to keep the ring.

Postponing The Big Day

Things will be easier to sort out if you are just postponing the wedding day for various reasons (illness, a death in the family, losing your job). It will be easier to negotiate with wedding suppliers if they know that they will still get your custom further down the line.

Marrying Abroad

Marrying abroad is obviously going to be more complicated than marrying in your own country. Some guests may not be able to make it however, or may resent paying the airfare.

CHAPTER 4: VENUES

Making the right choice for your wedding venue is one of the most important wedding decisions you will make. It will also probably be the most expensive.

When choosing a venue think about where your family and friends are located and then plonk your venue in the middle, or at least in a location which will be easy for everyone to get to. We got married in London and I was devastated when I found out how many of my Scottish family would not be able to attend. If you plan far enough in advance this may not be a problem though. So the things to think about are:

Location: the easiest way to narrow down your search is by deciding where you want to get married. Then you can search for venues in that area. That may still leave you with a lot of choice. You could also just want to choose between town or country. You may want to get married in your childhood church but you will still need a reception venue. If your venue and ceremony venue are different also take transportation into account.

An overseas wedding is another option and see Chapter 2 for more details

Price: don't look at venues outside of your budget because if you then fall in love with one it will hurt and everything else will feel like second best. Most venues are expensive but it is possible to find a beautiful one that will not break the bank.

What are they offering? Some venues, such as a marquee, come 'dry'. Which means with nothing at all and you have to get the furniture and even the electricity yourself. Other venues offer packages that are all-inclusive and most offer something in-between. When choosing your venue think carefully about what they offer. Our venue offered china, cutlery, napkins, glassware, a cake stand and knife, a master of ceremonies, linen and a venue planner. All of this stuff really came in handy and saved us a fortune because otherwise we would have had to rent it.

If you are having a civil ceremony then you can get married and have your reception in the same venue. If you are having a religious wedding however then you will also need a reception venue. Keep in mind that you can only get married in a licensed venue so if the venue you have your heart set on doesn't have one then you will have to get married elsewhere and then have your reception there, or a proper legal ceremony later. If you are having a civil ceremony and want to have a separate reception venue then take the expense and time of travel into account if you decide to do this.

Anyone who has watched Don't Tell The Bride will know that there are many different ways to wed and a lot of different venue options. Couples have gotten married in a swimming pool in a leisure centre – yes, you read that right. The bride used to work there. Interesting episode. In a wood, on a plane…anywhere really, as long as you make the wedding legal afterwards and also have a reception venue if needed. hitched.com are great for finding wedding venues and your local councils website will have a list of licensed venues for civil ceremonies. Where you can legally marry has been covered in chapter two so I will focus on reception/civil venues here.

In fact, because you can have so many choices finding a venue can be overwhelming. Recommendations are always a good idea when choosing a venue. Ask friends and family and even use social media to your advantage by asking Twitter and Facebook friends if they have any recommendations. Try to have an idea of what you want in mind. Even what you don't want can help.

Getting married in a marquee is popular and can be truly wonderful for a summer wedding. You will have to hire the marquee dry however, most of them just come on their own and you have to supply the generator yourself. You could even get married in a friend's garden. This option would also allow you to involve any pets. Don't assume that getting married in a marquee or a piece of land will be cheaper.

If you have always had your heart set on a specific wedding venue then make sure you book it as quickly as possible. Many book up years in advance.

With a bit of homework you will find your perfect venue. Bridal magazines are a great source. The real weddings and the resources/advertisements are all valuable. There is also a bridal magazine called Wedding Venues & Services which has a large directory of venues which is listed by county. If you have already hired your caterer or another wedding supplier then they will have some recommendations of their own. Make sure their recommendations are valuable and not just a friend or someone who will give them a commission. The internet is obviously a brilliant way to find a wedding venue. Choose your search terms and then happy surfing. If you have your heart set on getting married in a historical venue then the National Trust website is your friend: www.nationaltrust.org.uk. The English Heritage site is also worth a look www.english-heritage.org.uk. Wedding fairs are also an excellent place to gather information and find your potential venue. Your local council website will also have a list of licensed venues. If you have seen a venue that you love check their website or give them a call to find out if they hold weddings. If you have a wedding planner they will have an endless list of possible venues and will be able to source more based on your preferences.

Marquee and Teepee.

Marquees are popular and you can get a number of different ones. They usually come dry i.e. completely empty, and you will have to provide everything including the electricity. Keep in mind that you cannot get married outdoors. You have to get married in a 'permanent structure' but you can still have your reception in a marquee. This is usually the case in all weddings apart from Jewish ones. A teepee is not one of those Native American homes but a tent that slopes on one side. It keeps out the rain but retains the view. These options can add up with lots of

hidden costs so prepare for that. It is not good if you are on a tight budget but is if you want everything your own way. It could work out cheaper however if you have access to a large kitchen as you could self-cater. You would also save on alcohol and corkage fees. However you may have to rent the following: loos, power generators, decoration and lighting. Also think about rain. Rain covers may cost extra but they will be worth it, as would making sure someone is on hand to deal with the electricity. The company you hire the marquee from should know everything you need to know. When planning, plan for the worst weather while
hoping for the best weather. If the portaloo is not near the marquee than hiring a covered walkway will keep guests happy. You don't want anyone getting soaked on your wedding day. Also have a think of how guests will get there and if they will have anywhere that they can park. If there will be neighbours warn them in advance or invite them. That should stop any moans. Keep in mind that the ground may be wet and muddy so you will need some flat shoes or wellingtons. Keep disabled guests in mind. Make sure they will be comfortable in the marquee, are near a heater and can get around conveniently.

Castles

Possible if you have the budget. Make sure you can dine inside otherwise you may also have to hire a marquee.

Manor House

There are some truly gorgeous manor houses out there. The catering is usually in-house. Many of them come with wedding coordinators who will help deal with suppliers and make sure the day goes smoothly.

Hotel

There are a lot of very beautiful hotels around. Some of them will also give inclusive deals which can work out a lot cheaper than hiring other venues that seem to cost less at first glance.

Barns

I have seen some beautiful weddings set in barns. As with marquees, many will allow you to bring in your own food and alcohol which can keep costs down. Decoration costs may add up however but food and alcohol are a much bigger wedding expense.

There are some very unique places you can hire: boats, museums, galleries, woods. The list goes on. Many A-listers like Reese Witherspoon get married in their own garden. Which is fine if you own a multi-million pound home. Angelina Jolie and Brad Pitt got married at their holiday home in France. Be creative with your choices and think outside the box.

When booking a venue make sure you go through every bit of paperwork with a fine tooth comb. Check every single detail and if you are not sure about something then ask. Make sure the date is correct, little mistakes can cost big. Make sure the contract includes the full price, what is included, the deposit paid, the payment terms, when the rest of the balance is due, location, cancellation date, the details of the person you will be dealing with and the date and time of your wedding. If you have negotiated any deals or extras with the venue then make sure these are included in the contract. Some venues will let you pay the deposit in chunks and then the remainder before the wedding. Others will just want a reasonable deposit and send an invoice after the wedding. I would advise against paying 100% of anything far in advance. That should set off warning bells. Don't sign anything you are unsure about and remember that you are the customer. It is your wedding day and your money. Be firm but polite with people. Email is a good course of communication as these can be reread and checked if any misunderstanding occur.

Don't take any family members to see the venue with you. You don't want them being critical or trying to sway your decision if you decide it is the venue for you. Yes, even if they are paying for it or contributing. It is your wedding, not theirs. Don't be bullied.

Make notes when you go to the venue. Take the best man or maid of honour and check all of the rooms. Ask for a brochure, menus and the wine list. Make sure you can take pictures and do so if allowed. Even if you completely fall in love with the venue don't let them know. This will give you more bargaining power if they think you can just go somewhere else. Don't settle for second best either. When you see the venue that is the one you will know it.

What to know when choosing your wedding venue.

Questions to ask.

What does the package include?
How much alcohol do you provide, if any?
Do you have to go with their suppliers or can you choose your own?
Is there an extra charge if you do not go with their preferred supplier?
Can we bring in our own alcohol?
How much is your corkage fee?
What rooms do we have?
How long do we the venue for?
What is the hire fee?
Are there any additional charges?
If it is a hotel then ask if you get a deal if guests stay overnight.
What is the cancellation policy?
Are you allowed to use candles and will the venue supply them?
When can you or the suppliers decorate the venue?
How long do you have the venue for?

Are there any special offers they can give you? Especially for a mid-week or off-season weddings.

What is the venue capacity?

Is there a minimal amount on number of guests? You may have to pay an extra cost

Are all staff included in the price?

Will there be an event manager and/or master of ceremonies on the day?

How much is the deposit and when will the rest of the money have to be paid?

If you have fewer guests than their minimum numbers what will you be charged?

How many tables can you fit comfortably in the room you are having the wedding breakfast in?

Is there available parking space?

Is there disabled parking space?

Where can people get dressed and ready?

Do we have the venue exclusively?

Is there another wedding happening on the same day?

If catering and booze is in house then enquire about a price estimate.

Do you have a liquor licence?

Are you allowed to decorate the venue? What is, and is not, allowed?

How long does it take to turn the room?

When can suppliers have access to the venue?

When do things have to be collected?

Is there a contingency for bad weather?

Find out how much alcohol is supplied and if there are any extra charges.

What time does the venue's licence run out? What time do your guests have to be out by?

Who is the contact and who will be working at the venue on the day?

Are there any noise restrictions?

When you call up the venue initially make a note of how they treat you and how professional they are. If you are not impressed at the beginning it is unlikely to get any better. It sounds obvious but don't book the venue until you have seen it. When you go to view it have a proper look around. Try to spot any potential problems or anything that doesn't fit then discuss it with the venue in advance. Do your research on the venue before you sign anything. Check Facebook and Twitter. Search for reviews online and ask if they have any pictures of previous weddings. Take trusted members of your wedding party with you to see the venue again. They might spot something that you have missed. Write down any questions you will have in advance so you don't forget anything. Take a pen with you so you can write down any more questions that come to you.

When you go and see the venue they might show you the nicest rooms and they might not be done up how they are on the actual day. Make sure you know what is included and what is not. Some pictures on wedding venue sites are also of actual weddings and don't show the room as it is on the day. Watch out for this as it will add to your budget.

The advantages of hiring a dry venue is that you can make the venue your own and bring in your own food and alcohol. You will need to be very organised and it will take a lot of work. You can slash the cost dramatically however as food and alcohol are both very expensive. Check whether the venue has staff that will help on the day, if not you may have to do this yourself or hire someone separate. Also ask if you have to set up the chairs and clear up afterwards.

If the venue does in-house catering then ask for a tasting. Some venues do not hold tastings but if you are paying for catering then you should be allowed to make sure it is up to par. I understand this can be costly for the venue but catering bills are not cheap and you should be allowed to make sure that the food is good enough. Compare the in-house catering prices to the price of an outside caterer. Make sure you include any extra charge for going with an outside caterer and the cost of cutlery, china, napkins and linen if the venue will not supply these.

For a good deal it is best to either go inclusive or hire an inexpensive hall or function room.

The good thing about inclusive deals is that there won't be any surprises. If you want to get married quickly then you are in a strong bargaining position or if you want to get married off-peak. They won't want their room being empty. Make sure you know what you are getting. Break the price of the food and alcohol down per person to make sure you are getting a good deal. The venue will try and squeeze you so watch out for any hidden extras. Find out how much alcohol is included and what kind of wine they will be serving. Make sure it is not just some cheap wine and not limited to a certain number of bottles. Negotiate with the venue but makes sure it is for something that is worth it and really saves you money.

Venue And Reception In Different Places

This can be cause for stress so make sure everyone knows the route and exactly where they are going. Factor in how long it will take guests to get into their cars and travel or take the train/tube/bus. You may want to lay on transportation if the venue is far away or in the country. You don't want the reception running late. Or have taxis outside waiting for your guests.

My husband James and I got married at the London Rowing Club on Putney Embankment. It was a very good choice and not just because it is about ten minutes from our flat. All of our guests loved our venue. Sorry for being immodest but it really was a huge hit. Here I asked the venue and events manager, Olivia Malcolm Berry, to answer a few questions. Olivia is the one who deals with suppliers and makes sure everything goes smoothly on the day.

Tell us about the London Rowing Club.

Built in 1856, the London Rowing Club on the Embankment in Putney is one of the oldest rowing clubs in the world. The club still runs as a high performance rowing club, and hosts a number of important rowing events, such as the Oxford/Cambridge Boat Race Day. As a venue in London, the glorious panoramic views of the River Thames with Bishop's Park just across the water makes this idyllic location perfect for any event.

Why do people choose the London Rowing Club as a venue?

A main draw to the London Rowing Club are the 3 wonderful event rooms, and a large balcony that offers glorious panoramic views.
The club is also close to transport, is quite central, and when you have an event at the London Rowing Club you also have an experienced event manager to help organise your event.

How many weddings does the London Rowing Club do every year?

The Club hosts a range of different events, from rowing events such as Boat Race Day, to birthday parties and weddings. The club would host about 30 weddings a year.

What is your role?

I am the Venue and Events Manager for the club.

What kind of questions should a couple ask about a possible wedding venue?

1.   What capacity can the venue hold?

2.   Are there any limits to decorating?/ Can you have candles?

3.   Can you have live music, is there a restriction to the time they can play?

4.   Does the venue have a suppliers list? This can be a great way to find the suppliers you are after without the fuss of searching high and low. Their suppliers will also know the venue and the staff, making it a stress free event.

5.   If needed, does the venue allow children, have disabled access, is there any parking?

Any advice for how couples can decorate the venue?

Flowers always look fabulous, and are a wonderful way to dress up the venue. Once you have a colour scheme/theme for the day you can start planning any decorations for the venue. It is also good to see if the venue offer any decorations, candles etc.

Have you noticed any wedding trends?

Most of the weddings at the club are quite romantic, whimsical and rustic, as it all blends in quite nicely to the club.

What mistakes do couple make when planning a wedding?

The Wedding Survival Guide

Some couples are so worried about what their guests will think that they lose focus on what they want and how they want to spend the day. Don't worry about what everyone else is doing, this is your day!

Any good wedding planning tips?

Make sure you book the venue as soon as possible. Don't wait till the following year as prices increase, so the sooner you book the better.

What are the most important things to get right?

All couples are different, so their focus might be on the right meal or having the right wines/open bar available! The day is meant to reflect you as a couple though so as long as you and your guests are relaxed and having fun, that is the most important thing.

What is your favourite wedding you ever planned?

My favourite event would have to be one in the South of France, it was extravagant and divine!

Any tips for scheduling?

I think having a wedding folder and making lists are the best way to go about it, this will also help to keep track of contacts and budgets.

Thank you, Olivia.

SOME OTHER TIPS

Do Your Homework

Doing your homework will save money and also lead you to that perfect thing that makes your wedding. It can be time-consuming and hard to fit it into your life. Entire weekends and evening will have to be sacrificed but hopefully you will find some fun in it.

Decoration

It is your wedding and you can do it however you want. Bunting, a themed wedding, balloons, honeycombs, aliens…anything goes really. But do remember that it is a wedding and try to think of the end result. You don't want a mishmash.

Lighting.

Worth finding out if your venue will do anything during your first dance. It is nice if they dim the lights and then have some disco lights or something. Check the lighting in the venue. Especially if you are going to have your pictures done inside.

Tabletop

You can add whatever you want to the tabletop. It is hard to go wrong with flowers and candles however. You don't have to spend a fortune and if money is really tight then some candles and flower petals can really work. You also don't have to spend a fortune on flowers. That is just the 'W' bomb dropping again.

Chairs

Should come with the venue. If you have a marquee wedding you will have to supply your own. If you don't like the chairs at the venue you can hire chair covers. This is a popular thing to do and can really add a lovely touch.

Napkins

Check if venue supplies them. If not, you don't need to spend a fortune. Get some funky ones if you are having an informal wedding or some on eBay or Amazon if not.

Crockery and Cutlery

Check if the venue supplies these and, if so, if they charge. If they don't you will have to rent some from your caterer or somewhere else.

Menu

My (then) fiancé did our menus. He designed them himself with help from the internet and printed them out on good paper he bought from a stationery shop. Our guests loved them and they really did look great. You don't need to get them professionally done, this is an area where money can be saved.

Place Cards And Table Settings

Our place tags were luggage tags taped onto gourmet jelly bean favours. When it comes to place cards and table settings there are a lot of unique ways to add a bit of personality to the venue and make your guests feel special. You could have their name on a jar of something nice, a little plant pot of lavender, cubes, a tree stand or anything else that takes your fancy. You could even use the menu. A personalised menu with the date of your wedding and the guest's name is a nice memento.

Seating Plans

Despite the fact I am the one who is supposedly the artist in our marriage my husband also did the seating plan for our wedding. We were devastated when it went missing towards the end of the night. We wanted to keep it forever.

One way of doing it is drawing the different tables and then adding the names of the guests around the table. Get a good calligraphy pen and some good A1 or A2 card and you can do this yourself. Make sure you buy more than one sheet in case you make a mistake. You could also do one on your computer and then get it blown up at a print store. Seating plans look good propped on an easel.

Top Table

Ah, the top table. Where hearts are broken and war is waged. The top table is wherever the bride and groom sit. It can be terrifying doing the top table as so many people think they should be on it and some people have to be on it, even if they don't deserve it. The best thing to do is just make your decision and then stick to it. Explain to people, politely and firmly, why they are not on it if they complain. Giving them your reasoning and saying you would have liked them on it but just didn't have the space should suffice.

We could not fit our entire wedding party on our top table and we were quite upset about it initially but then we had the idea of having bridesmaids and best men on the other tables as our representatives. This actually worked very well, both for the guests at those tables who were with someone who knew what was going on, but also for us as we had emissaries at the other tables to sort out any issues and we could sit family members next to their partners and the best man and maid of honour next to theirs. It can be quite difficult when partners of the wedding party don't know anyone and have to sit alone whilst their other half is on the top table.

Divorced families can make doing the seating plan for the top table incredibly hard. The best thing to do is remind everyone that it is your big day and they should all be mature, get along and sit wherever they are told. Harsh but fair.

Traditionally in the UK the bride and groom sit in the middle of the table and then it is the bride's parents, then the groom's parents and then the best man and chief bridesmaid. With the divorce rate so high however (Shh! this is a wedding book!) this does not have to be followed at all. Sit whoever you want next to you and ignore all of the stuffy people who complain endlessly about tradition. Usually people only throw that word around during wedding planning when they are trying to get their own way anyway.

Either sit all parents at the top table or none. Otherwise you will offend people. If you do not sit your parents at your table, give them their own table which is relatively near you and surround them with family and friends. Then fill your own table up with the wedding party and/or your friends. Many people will say that the top table should be filled on one side only and clearly visible during the meal. However, few people want to be stared at whilst eating and not many like being put on display. Do what you want and sit where you want.

Make sure there is plenty of space around the tables and people can move freely. If you have ushers, or even just some lovely people who don't mind helping out, have them at the door, mini-seating plan in hand, ready to show people were they are supposed to be sitting. This will quicken the process. We did not have any problems on our wedding day, guests easily found their seats from the seating plan. You can number your tables in various creative ways: place card, plants, flowers, a number on a prop or a wooden number. You could also give the tables names instead. Even better if the name of each table is significant to you or the people who are sitting there. To make it even more personal you could name the tables after films you both like or places you have been on holiday together.

Obviously if you are having a themed wedding it will be much easier to decide what kind of place cards, decoration and favours you want. Pop your wedding theme into a search engine and you should have ideas aplenty.

Favours

For our wedding we got gourmet jelly beans. Which was quite funny when we had them delivered from Ocado. A favour can be anything and doesn't have to be expensive. They can be something special to you both as a couple or just a cute little trinket. Not On The High Street has some beautiful favours and eBay also has a lot of bargains. Supermarkets should not be discounted as edible favours are usually well received. Most people don't want something useless that they will feel obliged to keep. Some great ideas for favours are: sugared almonds, a little plant pot with a beautiful flower, herb or plant in. Personalise them and if you give a herb maybe add one of your favourite recipes too. Terracotta pots are very cute and look good. Miniature cake, chocolate, homemade cookies or cupcakes, a CD of your wedding playlist, your own personalised perfume, your own blend of tea, a book of love poems or quotes, alcohol, homemade chutney or jam, macaroons or champagne flutes. The list is endless but do make it personal. Guests will appreciate you making an effort. If you are not putting the favours on the tables before the wedding breakfast then put them in paper bags with the gift wrapped in tissue paper. Have them at the door with clear instructions to take one or have a member of the wedding party give them out.

CHAPTER 5: GUEST LIST AND INVITATIONS.

The first thing you will notice about wedding invitations is how expensive they are. If you buy them from John Lewis or any of those places they cost quite a bit of money. Don't get discouraged though because you can buy beautiful, personalised invitations at a very good price. You could also make your own. Although that might cost more and be time-consuming.

Invitations are traditionally sent six weeks before the wedding but I would email/call or send a save the date card three to four months beforehand. If you are getting married on a bank holiday or when people would be away this is even more important. Send invitations to guests who live abroad in plenty of time. They might not get them or it might just take a while.

On the save the date cards put your name, the date and the place and that the invitation/full details will follow. If you don't want to send cards and have some spare cash then you can buy lots of cute things like magnets as a save-the-date reminder. Wedding websites have a lot of very cute things.

Think about how many invitations you will need carefully. Although it is good to have some extra a common mistake is to think that because you have 120 guest that you need 120 invitations. There will be many couples and they will only need one invitation. The same for families.

Now a lot of wedding invitations are incredibly expensive. You are talking hundreds of pounds for a piece of cardboard. We were shocked at the prices. If you add in save the date cards and thank you cards, it would be easy to rack up a thousand pounds if you include postage. So what is a frugal girl to do? Ebay. Obviously. We got beautiful, personalised invitations for a very reasonable price. The invitations are beautiful, come with envelopes and are well made and high quality. Just put 'wedding invitations' into the search function of eBay and you can get some amazing ones for under £50.

We didn't send out save the date cards because of environmental reasons, and also cost. We emailed and called people instead. The wedding industry is a £10 billion industry in the UK so don't buy something just because you feel you have to. When it came to the design of our invitations, we wanted something that reflected us and who we are. Family members will probably try and pull you in a certain way, but we wanted ours to be fresh and fun. Our invites are white, with a multicoloured tree. We are quite a young couple so we wanted something to reflect that: nothing stuffy. They also came in a very handy, protective plastic case.

If you want to spend more on your invitations then John Lewis do some beautiful ones, and so do Marks and Spencers and VistaPrint. Watch out with VistaPrint though. I once bought some business cards on VistaPrint and somehow signed up to something that took £9.99 from my bank account every month. It took me a few months to notice and I was very angry. Thankfully when I called them up they were nice and I got my money back. I have since bought some more business cards from them with no problems. If you are good at DIY you can also make your own. Your computer will probably have some software that will allow you to do invitations. There are also plenty of good templates online. If you want to make your wedding invites last longer and you are willing to spend a bit more you can print your invite on something long-lasting like a tea towel or a coaster.

What to put on your invites

Your names (we included our surnames as we weren't sure people would know who we were!)
Date and time of the wedding.
Contact details. We asked people to RSVP to our email or by calling. You can include an RSVP card and envelope (with a stamp) or include your address. We wanted to keep our invitations as brief as possible.
RSVP details. Include a non-email option for the older guests. Include a deadline for the RSVP. Needed for the catering and seating. We made the mistake of putting an RSVP date which was too early. Some of our poor guests probably got their card after the date on them. Cue apologies. We had a lot of people who we would have loved to have come but only a limited amount of spaces so we wanted to hurry things up. Little did we know how long some people would take to reply. Typically, your RSVP by date should be three-to-four weeks before the wedding.

RSVP comes from the French Répondez, s'il vous plaît which means, respond (if you please).

RSVP cards for weddings should never have a place for number of guests. Your guests should know that only those addressed in the envelope are invited.
Include the venue address and the reception address too if it is different.
Your wedding gift list number. We went with John Lewis and prezola.com

Other options

Parents' details. We decided not to do this but you can include either parents or both. As in: 'Mr and Mrs Smith invite *guest name* to the marriage of their daughter, Chloe, to Matt Fox.'

Dress code.
Traditionally you don't put a dress code on wedding invitations. We didn't put one on as everyone knows weddings are formal. I would only include a dress code if it is anything other than formal. For instance: a themed wedding or black tie. Some guests won't like this however. We did get one or two emails from people wondering what to wear. If I did it again I might put a dress code on the invitations even though it is not the done thing.

Dietary requirements: You may want to enquire about this on the invitation. We did so on our save-the-date emails/calls.

Maps: good if you are getting married in the middle of nowhere.

Accommodations details: With information on special rates, good hotels and contact details.

You can, of course, put whatever you want on your invitations. It is your wedding.

Typeface and Font

Have a look at lots of different ones. They are a lot of choose from. One will suit your personality and wedding perfectly.

Paper

Having your invitations printed on good paper makes all of the difference. It doesn't need to cost a fortune.

Making Your Own

You can make and design your own invitations. There are also many templates on-line that can help and most computers even come with decent design software.

One of the most important things is to proof your wedding invitations. Spelling mistakes and bad grammar are not good. Check and double check yourself and get someone else too as well. When you get your proof back from the printer you can still make changes at no extra cost.

Posting

Weddings are expensive so as long as you send them out in plenty of time guests shouldn't mind if you send the invitations second class. The Royal Mail's prices these days are pretty much extortion.

In regard to addressing envelopes, Debrett's may say to address married couples as Mr and Mrs John Smith, and it may be the done thing, but this is 2014, not the 1950s and I, and many of my friends, find it sexist and offensive. It is a tradition that really should die out. Always make sure the wife has her first name on and also make sure that she actually changed her name.

Putting Together Your Gift List.

We were not going to do a gift list but many of our guests asked us to because they just didn't know what gift to get. The best way to put together a gift list is to do an inventory of things you need. This can also include upgrades of things you have that are not very good: irons, kettles or toasters for example.

Write down your shopping list before you go to the store or log in online. It will be very annoying if you really need new towels but you didn't do a proper inventory or make a list.

When making your list keep in mind the financial situation of your guests. Not everyone will be loaded and they will also have to pay for transport, clothes and shoes to your wedding. Have a wide range of products with low to medium price tags. You could add one or two big purchases for a rich uncle but keep in mind that you don't want to look greedy and that most people won't have much to spend.

A number of things starting from £15 is a good idea. If you get a gift you don't want then either exchange it or regift. If you do regift it make sure the person who bought it for you doesn't know that person. That could get awkward. Many couples also sell their unwanted wedding gifts on eBay or other auction sites like Ebid.

John Lewis

My husband and I did our gift list through John Lewis (Peter Jones, the Sloane Square branch to be more precise) and our honeymoon fund via Prezola.

We have absolutely nothing bad to say about John Lewis. Their customer service is amazing, as are their products.

It is a lot of fun doing your gift list. You get given a scanner after you register and a voucher that gives you and your fiancé a free tea or coffee and a pastry. My first tip is not to wait too long to use your voucher as by the time we went to get our free pastry, not much was left. Although we did have a great bakewell tart and a cup of tea.

You then take the scanner and scan the barcode of the products that you want. You may have seen this done in numerous American romantic comedies. I had which is why I got stupidly excited. We got a little carried away and scanned far too much stuff we didn't need, including a £45 (!) chopping board. It doesn't matter if you do this as you can just remove the items online. Or add more of course. You can't add sale items however as they may not be available by the time you get married. The return policy at John Lewis is very good. You just have to give your gift list number. They will post you a summary at the end. Keep this incase anything becomes faulty.

Prezola

My fiancé and I were quite sick of how much stuff we had in our flat. We are both also quite environmentally conscious and didn't want to end up with a lot of stuff we had nowhere to put. Add in the fact that weddings are expensive and we decided that we would tell guests we would prefer a contribution to our honeymoon fund rather than more stuff. Our guests were understanding and didn't mind so you can look into this option. If anyone does want to buy you a gift you keep for the rest of your life then you can add some gifts from Prezola (they have lots of beautiful things) or add a separate gift list such as John Lewis or Debenhams.

I found out about Prezola in the wedding magazines I bought in the flush of my engagement. I made sure I researched it thoroughly before my (then) fiancé and I paid the £25 you need to pay if you want the honeymoon fund. If you just want the gift list it is free.

We didn't have a problem with Prezola. They didn't transfer the money immediately after the wedding but did within three or four business days after I contacted them asking how we close the list and get the funds. They were also very friendly and give you a spreadsheet of wonderful wedding messages along with the name of the guest and their gift. I can recommend Prezola.

Some guests didn't want to put their financial details on the internet and put their honeymoon contribution straight into our bank accounts instead.

Of course there are other options for gift lists: art, a contribution to your favourite charity, things like a massage or spa breaks or an experience. The opportunities are endless. Search online if you don't want to go with a typical department store.

Thank You Cards

It is best to make a note or who gave you what or write your thank you cards immediately. It may be a bore but you will thank yourself for it later. Although not everyone sends thank you cards these days, after your wedding it is a personal touch that your guests really will appreciate. Some beautiful paper or some nice cards make a great touch. Make sure you personally thank your guest for their gift and add in some nice, personal comments.

Thank you cards can be very expensive but Paperchase and WH Smith tend to do them in packs of ten starting from £3.99. This can add up if you had a lot of guests. There will be a few that are £2.99 for ten or you could buy some good paper and envelopes. This might work out cheaper due to volume. Marks & Spencer also do some beautiful ones at only £2.50 for eight.

Who To Invite

Now, this is a hard one. Decide on numbers first then it will be easier to make the hard decisions, knowing that you only have a certain amount of places.

Doing The Guestlist

Not every person you invite will come to the wedding. Send your save the date cards or emails and get a feel of the numbers. Then you can start inviting other people. People who are not on the first list, if they find out, will hopefully know that there are people that you have to invite and they are not on the B-list.

Day Guests

Day guests will be there from the ceremony to the evening. You will have to feed them and buy them alcohol so you may need to limit their numbers if you are on a budget.

Evening Guests

You can also invite evening guests. Perfect for those who cannot come during the day or for people like work colleagues that you just don't know very well. Do not, however, expect evening guests to buy you an expensive gift. Wedding gifts are traditionally supposed to cover the cost of the meal.

You may be under pressure from people to invite certain people that you might not want to your wedding. The family friend that you met a few times, a distant cousin....I was lucky as my parents are very understanding and knew our wedding was only about James and me. They also knew we were not rich and didn't want a big wedding anyway. They never insisted any of their friends be there. If you are not so lucky then listen to the reasons that person wants a certain person there. If they have a point and you have the space, fine. If not, kindly remind them that it is *your wedding* not a social event for them and their friends. There were a few people my husband and I wanted at our wedding who we couldn't have there. So think careful-ly before you send out any invitations or get bullied into doing anything. My top tip is invite the people you truly love who make a huge difference to your life first. Your wedding day should be full of people who will be friends for life and see you through thick and thin, and family members that you have no option but to invite. Only jok-ing, but do make your decisions carefully.

Another thing to keep in mind is that some people will take it very personally if you do not invite them to your wedding. In fact, they might never speak to you again. If this matters to you, invite them. If not, nothing is lost.

CHAPTER 6: HEN AND STAG DO

Before you and your beloved commit to each other for life tradition dictates that you have 'one last night of freedom'. This may not be just a day but, in some cases, a week.

Hen Night

Your maid of honour/chief bridesmaid will arrange and plan your hen night. Make her job easier by giving her a full list of people you want to come with full contact details, along with some ideas of likes and dislikes.

My chief bridesmaid, Paloma, did a 'Catherine Quiz' to get a hold of my likes and dislikes and then planned an amazing hen night. It started with an afternoon tea/ champagne party and then ended the night in a London casino. It was amazing and fun.

There are great sites which can help you organise the hen/stag dos. Just type 'stag do' or 'hen do' into a search engine and you will get ideas galore.

Some things to do on a hen night include a spa break, cocktail making, a pyjama party, afternoon tea, a night in a casino, a movie marathon, wine tasting or a boat ride. The stag do is much the same deal. The best man arranges it.

Stag Night

Not always the *Hangover* cliché but do make sure that it happens weeks, if not months, before the wedding. Otherwise bad things will happen. Much like the hen do, the best man will need a list of people and their contact details. Then he will need some likes and dislikes. The best man may know exactly what would make the ideal stag do but some ideas always help.

Weekend breaks in Europe are popular, water rafting, paint balling, motor racing and SAS training are all good, fun ideas.

For some great advice read my interview with Tom Wright who was my husband's best man on our wedding day. Tom was an amazing best man and he really went beyond the normal duties of a best man, helping my husband get well and actually make it to the ceremony.

How did it feel to be chosen as the best man?

Once I got over the initial surprise I felt very honoured. I know from meeting Jamie's friends on the stag that he had plenty of fantastic options to choose from. I also felt a great responsibility to try and live up to that faith he'd put in me.

Was it stressful?

Planning things was, but that was my own fault. I'm terrible at starting tasks, so I was pushing things pretty close to the wire with speech writing and stag planning. Made things more stressful than they needed to be! Thank god for Kaedi telling me to just bloody start.

What was the hardest thing about it?

Other than seeing Jamie in pain on the day, it was as mentioned above, starting the stag planning/speech writing. It didn't help that I didn't have a full list of people coming for a while (thanks Jamie!), but that was my responsibility so should've pushed him a bit more there.

And the easiest?

Actually doing stuff! The stag was fantastic, everyone wanted it to be a great night so that's what it turned out as.

Giving the speech was much easier than I'd feared. After the morning of seeing Jamie get through what he had, my nerves had disappeared. I was more worried about dropping the rings than giving the speech!

How did you decide what to do for the stag do?

Since I didn't know the majority of the guys coming on the stag I had went for things I thought everyone could enjoy, while trying to stay within the London area. I also wanted to keep things relatively cheap as I wasn't sure everyone was employed etc.

I had toyed with the idea of 'adventure days' but thought they would cause a lot of hassle with people getting out of London, and be very expensive. For me the main part of the day would be the evening meal and drinks after. So I went with the Urban Golf for the activity, easy to get to, relatively cheap, easy fun for everyone, and drinks available as soon as you walk in!

How much planning was required?

The stag was the culmination of about 2-3 weeks thinking on it, and then a day ringing around places booking stuff up.

The speech was a furious 2-3 hour session the night after the stag. I practiced in front of Kaedi and my mum about 5-6 times until I knew it by heart. They also helped me cut parts out which were dull and kept it flowing.

Were you nervous?

Not really, once the planning was done it was smooth sailing for me.

How was the wedding day?

It was absolutely lovely. The service was beautiful, not to mention the location which really stood out at sunset. I had a fantastic time meeting everyone, including your lovely family!

Obviously it was very sad that you and Jamie had to leave early, but I was so impressed with you both on the day. I can really see why you two make a great married couple.

What are your top Best Man Tips?

Don't put things off, as is true with everything in life it just introduces more stress than there should be.

Practice your speech a load of times, and get feedback on the best/worst parts. Try and make sure you can recite it from heart

Any tips for making the speech?

Talk to the groom about your past experiences together with the aim of getting some good stories for the speech. You can also get the other guys on the stag to do the same thing. I recently went on another stag do, and at dinner we went around the table each giving one amusing story involving the stag and the person giving the story, as well as one word to describe the stag. Was a great idea!

I made a list of qualities about Jamie, and a list of stories I had, and then tried to weave the best into the speech.

Thank you, Tom

Who Pays?

That is the question. Generally, and traditionally, neither the hen nor stag are supposed to pay anything towards their last night of freedom. The other hens and stags do. However, not everyone has a lot of money and it is worth offering to pay something. I bought a round of drinks on my hen night as all of my hens, and my chief bridesmaid in particular, had made such an effort. This only seemed fair.

Engagement Party

Some people have an engagement party. My husband and I didn't have one but I wish we had. You could do whatever you want for your engagement party but re serving an area in a favourite bar/club with some drinks and nibbles is a popular choice. Don't invite anyone to the engagement party who is not invited to the wedding. They will wonder what they did to offend you. The only way around that is if you are having a small wedding but be honest with people and make that clear.

If there is someone you don't want to invite to the engagement party then don't. Say you just had a small gathering with friends and ask people not to put the pictures on Facebook. Problem solved.

You don't have to pay for the engagement party but you could get some drinks and nibbles which I am sure would be appreciated. Presents are generally not given at engagement parties but if you do get one then remember to send a thank you card.

CHAPTER 7: TRANSPORT

There are a number of good options for transportation. Most are quite expensive however.

If you have a relative or friend with a decent looking car then you can get wedding car decoration kits that will make the car look amazing. My parents did this and when I saw the car I was so emotional and it looked amazing. They had used white ribbon on the outside along with some bows. On the inside they had draped all of the seats and the back in white satin and there were rosebuds and flowers on the back. It truly was beautiful. You can buy wedding car kits from eBay and in wedding stores.

Taxi

You could also take a taxi to and from your wedding. Just make sure the driver knows the importance of the event. You could even ask them to add a ribbon and bow. Just give them a big tip or hire them out for a few hours. If you are going to need a lot of taxis for guests at some point it helps to contact a local cab firm and then they can arrange for taxis to be outside for the guests. You don't want a mad scramble or guests being late.

Hiring a Car

If money is no object then you can hire the car of your dreams. Just make sure your wedding dress will fit into it. A classic car or a sports car can certainly add class to your day. A horse and carriage is popular and yet still unique. You could also hire a double decker bus which will have the name of you and your spouse on. This is also good if you have to transport guests. Not all of them will have transport themselves so it is always a good idea to lay some on if the ceremony and reception are in different places. If money is too tight to put on transport then you could ask guests who have cars to give those who don't a lift. They shouldn't mind.

Always factor in extra time when travelling on your wedding day. Country lanes have tractors and cities have traffic. Both have to be taken into account. If you can do the journey in advance on the same day and at the same time that your wedding would be. Also make sure there are no football games or other special events around the time of your wedding that could hold things up. See if there are alternative routes too. That should ease some stress just in case things start running late. Something else to consider is parking. Make sure there is enough and that guests know where parking is located.

CHAPTER 8: SCHEDULING.

Your wedding does not need to be strict and have every second planned out but you will need a running order. Don't panic, it is easier than it sounds.

First of all: you should choose who you want to be around you in the morning. As should your other half.

A rough running order would go like this:

Preparation.
Guests Arrive.
Ceremony
Drinks Reception
Pictures
Wedding Breakfast
Speeches
Cutting The Cake
First Dance
Dancing.
People Disperse.

You don't need to plan things to the minute unless you want to. This was my wedding schedule. It didn't go entirely to schedule, I was late *(bride's prerogative)* and I think the reception ran over a little but no one is going to notice if it doesn't run to the minute. Before the ceremony I had a makeup artist and my maid of honour and a bridesmaid come to my flat and we got ready. In fact, it ended up being quite the party as my husband was ill and we got the best man and his girlfriend to come along too! I may be the only bride to get ready when her husband-to-be was in the flat. I didn't put the dress on until he had left though.

An important note: make sure there is food for the wedding party. You don't want anyone fainting and it is a long day. There will also probably be champagne and the first glass might do some damage on an empty stomach.

Ceremony and Wedding Reception of Catherine & James

Deliveries the day before: Seating chart, table names, flowers, sparkling, jelly beans.

Wedding Day

2-2.30: Flowers

15:30 James and Guests arrive at LRC

15:45 Guests seated in Long Room

The Wedding Survival Guide

James interviewed by Registrar

15:50 Catherine arrives at LRC Catherine meeting with registrar

16:00 Ceremony commences. Lute played.

16:30 Ceremony ends

Reception Drinks – tea/coffee by LRC. Sparkling Elderflower.

Photographs

17:30 Cut the cake (it will be dessert)

18:00 Call to dinner

Couple announced by family

Ice water and white/red wine on each table

Starter

Main

Cake as dessert

18:30 Speeches x4 Prosecco served

20:00 Tea & Coffee in the Fairbairn Room DJ sets up

21:00 First Dance

23:00 Balcony closed

00:00 Carriages

Notes:

Prosecco station at the end of the bar with Red/White

4 round tables, 20 people on the long table

Who Should Have The Running Order?

Guests might appreciate a running order to know what is going on. At the very least make sure the key members of the wedding party have a running order so they can help the day go smoothly. Key people to have a running order are: maid of honour, best man, ushers, bridesmaids, father of the bride, mother of the bride, other family members, the venue, photographer, wedding planner etc. Although if you have a wedding planner or a venue coordinator they usually do the schedule for you, and should do too.

Make sure all of your suppliers have a copy of your schedule. Send it to them before the wedding just to make sure everything is okay and that they know what they are doing.

Schedule

Doing the schedule might be a nightmare. We were lucky as we had the venue manager do this for us. We had a say in it of course and ran through it with her but she did the final draft. This was a huge strain taken off. Things to include on the schedule are: the name and contact details of suppliers and key wedding party members, transportation details, timing (doesn't have to be 100% accurate), any specifics and any important details. If you don't have a wedding planner or venue coordinator then give the schedule to the maid of honour or an usher so they can manage it all and make sure everything goes according to plan.

Some people still have receiving lines but these are becoming unfashionable, especially as they take so long. If you have a small wedding then greeting people won't take up too much time but if not then you can have yourself announced into the room. This will mean that you don't greet every guest but you can make your rounds at the reception. You will also have more time to speak to people that way and won't feel rushed.

Weather checking

Checking the weather can become an obsession for a bride and groom, especially if you are having an outdoor wedding. There are plenty of apps to do so but try to not get too worried or obsessed.

DOING THINGS YOUR WAY

Vows

You can write your own vows if you want but there will be certain words that have to be said legally as the vows are part of a legal contract.

Readings

You can include readings in your vows. You could do your own readings or get a member of the wedding party to do one. These can be a poem or a passage from a book. Anything at all. You can even write your own.

Speeches

Traditionally the father of the bride goes first, then the groom and then the best man. I made sure my chief bridesmaid made a speech because otherwise it is just all men talking and is a bit sexist.

The speeches can go on for a while. An average of forty minutes. It is best if people have about 10 minutes each and then the groom can have longer. It is best if people don't ramble on too long. We served the food before the speeches and this is always a good idea. Otherwise people get drink on an empty stomach and the speeches might go on to the sound of rumbling stomachs. Champagne on an empty stomach is never a good idea either.

Some good tips if you are working on a speech: Start by writing some thoughts and stories down and then you can work the rest of the speech around those main stories. Childhood stories or a funny anecdote are great. There can be a trend to embarrass but it really is better not to. For grooms: don't forget to say how beautiful the bride is looking. Brides: don't be shy about mentioning certain things to the groom you want him to mention, whether it be where the wine is from or something nice about a family member. With the best man and maid of honour, let them know if you would like them to mention anything.

It is best to write the speech down in full, even if you don't want to copy it word-for-word. This will also help trigger the points you want to make. My poor dad forgot his speech in the chaos which was our wedding morning and had to wing it. Even if things do go wrong, remember the people in the room don't want you to fail. No one will find it amusing nor be rude. Funny is always a good idea but hold back on rude and inappropriate stories. There will be older relatives in the room. Another key point is to hold back on the alcohol until you do your speech. A drunk speech is never a good idea. Funny, but not a good idea.

CHAPTER 9: THE DRESS AND OTHER OUTFITS.

Yes, I have called this chapter: The Dress And Other Outfits. Because, let's be honest, the bride's dress is one of the most talked about things at a wedding. It is also usually the most expensive. The dress sets the tone and is very important. Don't stress though, you will find the perfect dress for you and your personality. As will the groom and the rest of the bridal party.

THE DRESS

What every little girl dreams about: her wedding dress. Wedding dresses tend to bring out the girly side of even the most tomboyish women. There is just something about the wedding dress that is iconic. There is a lot of pressure to get it right however. This can feel overwhelming. The best thing to remember is that it is your wedding dress, it doesn't matter if anyone else likes it or not. This is easier said than done and I was worried whether people would like my dress or not. In the end I made the right decision but it can be nerve-racking wondering what people's reactions will be, especially your fiancé's reaction. My now husband is notoriously fussy and when we looked at some wedding dresses together we both hated all of them. Luckily I was fussy too but when my husband said before our wedding that he hoped the dress was strapless and showed off my shoulders I did have a moment of panic. Thankfully he loved it on the day.

When choosing a dress go with your instincts. If a dress really grabs you and makes you emotional it is the right one. My dress made my mum, dad and brother cry. That is when I knew I had to buy it. When you start trying on wedding dresses that is when you realise that you are going to be a bride. It was the first time it hit me: 'I'm getting married'. It is a wonderful moment. Made even better when you buy your dress with your mother and/or bridesmaids.

Your wedding dress will probably be the most expensive item of clothing in your wardrobe. Well, unless you are very lucky. My wedding dress is one of the most expensive things I own. Your wedding dress is also significant as it symbolises a new phase in your life but if you just remember two things when you are buying your wedding dress you can't go wrong. 1) Make sure it suits you, your personality and your body shape. 2) Make sure you love it. Done. The wedding dress which is 'The One' is the one you are happiest in.

Deciding On Your Style

You will have a style in mind but be open to different dresses. When I saw my wedding dress on the hanger I liked it enough to try it on but I never thought it would be 'The One'. But when I tried it on everything slotted into place. I think this is the thing with most wedding dresses: you have to see them on, not on the hanger.

When deciding on the style of your wedding dress keep the venue and the season in mind. Even though I said that: do not be scared to buy an extravagant wedding dress. This is your wedding and your day. There are not many opportunities in life to dress up and even less to wear a beautiful, expensive dress with a train or one that billows. You don't have to get married in Westminster Cathedral to wear a dress worthy of a bride. Weather is something you can factor in. You might want to have a summery dress for hot weather or add a fake fur stole in winter. Good fabrics for a winter wedding are velvets, brocades and satins. A crepe dress works well in hot weather as would a light and floaty dress. For a casual day time wedding a suit can look truly beautiful and classy. You could jazz it up with heels, a hat and a beaded top if you wanted.

Another thing to keep in mind is that guests will spend a lot of time looking at the back of your dress. You might want to make sure that it is not too plain and has some detail. A lot of wedding dresses tend to be quite plain and then be extravagant at the back. You can do this in a number of ways. One way is with a train. There are a number of options for a train. The bridal train can look absolutely stunning and make you feel incredibly special. If you are getting married in a church you can have a long train but if you are getting married in a register office you might want a shorter one.

These are your train options:

Sweep: this is the shortest option. It just brushes the floor.
Chapel: 1-1.5 metres from the hemline.
Cathedral: 2.75 metres from the waist.
Royal Cathedral: extends 2.74 metres from the waist. Can go up to 7.62 metres.

Your seamstress will be able to put a button on your wedding dress or a hook so you can turn your train into a bustle. This is a good option, especially for when you are dancing. People tend to stand on trains and dealing with one all day may be too much. Most wedding dresses also have a hook of fabric underneath the skirt of the dress which you can loop around your dress. I had a train on my wedding dress and I loved it. It made me feel amazing and it looked great in pictures. I had a thread hook put half way up my dress and a button put near the bottom. This made it into a bustle and looked great. It gave the dress a completely different look and it also had a fabric hook on the underside of the skirt. Unfortunately the dress seemed to keep unhooking when I buttoned it and I gathered the skirt and carried it in the crook of my elbow. I liked how it felt doing this and it looked good in the pictures. It feels very grand and is show-stopping. You could also put the hook near the waist so the train will look sleeker when it is up. This ruined the line of the front of my dress so I had the hook half way up. It is a good idea to take a bridesmaid to your last fitting as it can be hard to figure out how to put the train up. I didn't and it took two guests quite a while to figure out how to do it.

If you are having a train your dress really should be floor length. You could go for a mullet look of course, but those are hard to pull off. Wedding dresses can be any length, most are floor length but do whatever you want. Do keep your height and the shoes you will be wearing in mind though. You don't want to look squat on your wedding day.

Floor length is standard but there is a trend for 1950s style wedding dresses which are knee length. Here are your length options:

Full Length: self-explanatory but the tip of your shoes should be visible and the dress should not be too long in the back that it can be stood on. You should be able to dance in a full length wedding dress without tripping over.

Mullet: shorter in the front and longer in the back. Can actually look very nice. Perfect for showing off your shoes.

Mid-length: otherwise known as knee length. Covers the knees.

Mini: a brave look for a wedding dress. Above the knee or shorter. The new mother-in-law probably won't be a fan.

Ballerina: Usually a fuller skirt that stops just above the ankles.

Tea-length: calf-length. Can be very flattering, depending on height and heel height.

Neckline

When thinking about necklines it helps if you keep your bust size in mind. I didn't go for a strapless wedding dress as I would have spent the rest of the day worried I would fall out of it. This probably would not have happened with a well-made dress but to look beautiful on your wedding dress you have to be comfortable. Here are your neckline options:

Halter: Has a strap that goes around the neck. It is sexy and revealing but don't let that put you off, it can look absolutely stunning on a wedding dress. It is backless or has a keyhole back and is very comfortable. Works on women of all sizes. You will need a strapless bra to wear underneath.

Scoop: Is a rounded neckline. Like a scoop.

Strapless: a very popular choice of wedding dress. Possibly the most popular choice but I am only going on observation. This is when the neck and shoulders are completely bare. Will have a corset-like bodice or a fitted bustier.

Sweetheart: This looks like a heart. It is off-the-shoulder and dips in the middle to make a heart-shape. Looks very beautiful and glamorous.

V-Neck: Is in the shape of a V and goes down into a deep point.

One Shoulder: This is an asymmetrical look. One arm and shoulder is bare and the other has one strap or a sleeve. Can look elegant and dramatic.

Boat Neck: This look is high in the front and back and follows the line of the collar bone straight across. It looks a bit like a boat and will usually skim both shoulder blades.

Jewel: Looks like a necklace around the collar bone. It has a small curve at the base of the neck.

Silhouette

The best way to get a flattering dress is to get one with a silhouette that looks good on you. Here are the options:

A-Line: this flares from either the bust or the waist. It looks like the letter 'A' which is why it is so called. The A-Line silhouette suits pretty much everyone and is also sometimes called the princess line.

Empire: great for pregnant brides. The bodice is cropped and the waist ends below the bust line. This silhouette is very elongating and flattering. Works well if you are self-conscious about your waist and have big breasts. Can be sleeveless or short sleeved.

Slip: this is basically a long tank top. Perfect for beach or casual weddings. May be backless or cut on the bias. It is not usually embellished and looks very elegant.

Ball Gown: a ball gown will have a fitted corset and a full skirt. This is the classic princess/fairy tale wedding dress style. The waist can be nipped in at your natural waist or at your hips. Whatever is most flattering. The ball gown silhouette tends to touch the floor and really suits brides with small waists.

Mermaid: This is a figure hugging dress that flares below the knee. It looks like a mermaid's tail, hence the name. It is also called a fish tail. It shows off curves well but can be hard to walk in. Although it can make you feel very elegant and ladylike as you have to take small steps.

Trumpet: The trumpet silhouette is different from the mermaid as the skirt gradually flares about mid-thigh. It has a close-fitting bodice.

Sheath: a sheath dress drops to the floor in one narrow, unbroken line. It is close fitting. This is a popular choice with slim brides and it tends to look like an evening gown. Great for a 1920s look.

Vintage Dresses

Vintage means clothes made between 1920s and 1970s. Anything before that is antique.

Sleeves

Most wedding dresses are strapless and they are the most popular style in the United Kingdom. There were only a minimal amount of other options until Catherine Middleton became the Duchess of Cambridge in a Grace Kelly style, long-sleeved lace wedding dress in 2011. It is an elegant look which can look old fashioned but can also look beautiful and sexy. The variety of wedding dresses which now have sleeves has grown but can still be a little sparse. If you want to buy a wedding dress with long sleeves it is possible though, thanks to Kate.

Here are the sleeve options:

Three-Quarters: this is flattering and ends just after the elbow. Perfect if you want to hid your upper arms but also want to show some skin.

Cap: a cap sleeve barely covers the shoulders. It is short and fitted. It can look beautiful but doesn't suit everyone.

Balloon: Wide and puffy sleeve which is wrist-length. Is quite dated now but it may be your dream dress and if so, then you can make it work for you. A pouf sleeve is the one on Princess Diana's Elizabeth Emanuel designed iconic wedding dress, which at the time of writing is to be given to her son Prince Harry for his 30th birthday. What will he do with it I wonder? The pouf sleeve is different from the balloon sleeve as it is short and gathered and sometimes worn off-the-shoulder. It is a hard look to carry off.

Bat Wing: very dramatic. Think Morticia Addams in The Addams Family. Has a wide armhole and then it extends out from the waist and is tight at the wrist. Makes you look like a bat, hence the name.

T-Shirt: Longer than a cap sleeve and generally more loose unless fitted.

Juliet: Is a long sleeve which has a little pouf at the shoulder and then the rest is tapered. Quite an old-fashioned, Shakespearean look.

Fitted: generally long and fitted.

Bell: Think bell-bottom trousers. Narrow at the top and then flares at the bottom. A bit 1970s but can be beautiful and flattering.

Where To Shop

Let's get the bad news out of the way first: some bridal stores will charge you just to make an appointment and try on dresses. This can be up to £50 and you will only get it back if you buy a dress. This will obviously add up if you go to a number of stores and, to be honest, I would not pay to try on some dresses. Some bridal boutiques will supply champagne while you try on dresses, so it might be worth it if you and your bridal posse can drink your money back in champagne. I only half jest. If you can't hold your booze however, hold back or you could end up making an expensive drunk purchase. Buying the wrong dress in an alcoholic haze is not the best way to buy the perfect wedding dress.

First, where to go. Bridal stores and boutiques are always a good bet but you usually have to make an appointment. These can be found easily with a quick internet search. You have also probably spotted some where you live. Couture and designer. Sigh, if only. If you have this type of budget, go for it.

Sample sales are a great place to pick up a wedding dress. Pretty much all of the big -and small- designers do them. Stores also do sample sales. You could buy an amazing wedding dress at a discount of 25-50 per cent. Sample sale dresses are dresses which have been ordered and then cancelled or dresses that have been tried on. Some may have defects or have to be dry-cleaned but you could get your dream dress at half the price. The internet is always a good place to find things and wedding dresses are no exception. This is an area where you must be careful as you won't be able to try on the dress and if you buy one online and it does not fit or is not what you expected you might not be able to take it back. While buying one online can work I would go to the store and try it on. Or at least make sure you could get alterations done. There are always a good number of wedding dresses on eBay. You could pick up a bargain there but do be careful. Check the sellers feedback and postage costs. Ask them any questions at all, especially if there are any stains or marks on the dress. Paying via PayPal is also a good idea as then you will have buyer protection if anything goes wrong.

If you are creatively inclined you could also make your own dress. Don't do this unless you have the talent and skill to pull it off. Wedding shows and fairs will also have wedding dresses galore. They will usually charge you to attend but it can be worth it as there will be a lot of suppliers there and ideas. A lot of designers and bridal stores will be out in force at wedding shows.

Another option is to rent your dress. Anyone who has seen Don't Tell The Bride has probably watched in horror as the groom has had a bespoke suit made for him and his best men while renting the wedding dress for the poor bride. While renting wedding dresses is popular in America, rental stores are few and far between in the UK. Although some bridal stores will allow you to rent dresses if you ask them. It makes sense to rent a dress you are only going to wear once. My wedding dress just sits in my wardrobe. Although I do bring it out and look at it quite a lot. I don't think I could ever part with it. Maybe one day I will have a daughter.

Think of your budget first and be honest with the salespeople about how much money you have. Being prepared to negotiate also helps.

You can bring along pictures from magazines or some pictures on your iPad to give the salesperson an idea of what you want. You could also bring some fabric swatches too. It will help if you have a general idea of what you want in mind. Your Pinterest account may really come into its own at this point.

If you can don't buy the dress immediately. An impulse purchase is not a good idea when buying a wedding dress. Ask the shop if they could put the dress aside for twenty-four hours and then go back and make sure it is still the one you want. Also be careful of going wedding dress shopping with too many people. They may all have different opinions which might confuse you and make things worse. Of course, they could also all fall in love with the same dress so, makeup your own mind but make sure you take people that you trust. Don't be swayed by other people's opinions. You are the one who has to wear the dress and look at pictures of it for the rest of your life.

Wear appropriate underwear when wedding dress shopping. A white or nude strapless bra, big pants (for modesty!) and some tights or leggings (also for modesty) are all good ideas. You will be changing in front of a completely stranger who will probably have to help you into the dress, as well as your friends or family. You might want to make sure the pants are seam-free and bring a pair of heels. Make sure the heels are comfortable and that you can walk in them.

The salespeople might use some bridal lingo. If you don't know what something means, ask. People who work outside the wedding industry won't know what certain things mean. Me included.

Many bridal stores will not allow you to take pictures of the dress for 'copyright reasons'. This is very annoying but they will allow you to take pictures if you purchase the dress, assuming it then has to be made. When I bought my dress I picked one and then it was made from scratch to my exact measurements. I could ask for changes and alterations. It took three months to finish and after it was I then had two fittings, the last one being two weeks before the wedding.

There are three ways in which you buy a wedding dress:

Bespoke: this is what I did. You make an appointment with the bridal store and try on their sample dresses. After you have chosen one your measurements will be taken and any other notes on changes you want to be made to the dress like adding sleeves or making the dress shorter. This will all be sent off to the designer and then the dress will be made. It will take about three months to make the dress and you will have to pay a deposit. You will then get the dress and any alterations will be noted and it will be sent to a seamstress to be fitted to your exact measurements. You should get at least two fittings. I had to pay an extra £200 on top of the price of my dress for the fittings. In hindsight, this was a bit much and I don't think I should have been charged the extra money. So watch out for hidden costs.

Off-the-peg: you go to the bridal store and choose a dress which is closest to your measurements and then the dress is altered to your exact size. This is a smart and economical option and if my mother and brother had not paid for my dress this is what I would have done.

Handmade: it makes no sense but this can actually be the cheapest option. If you go down this route then have a clear vision of what you want. There is nothing to try on and you will have to have a lot of confidence in your vision. Work with your dressmaker and know what fabric you want, how you want your dress to look on: the silhouette, length, bodice…make sure you know exactly what you want and allow plenty of time for any changes you might want made.

Second hand: when you buy a second hand wedding dress it has probably been worn for less than twelve hours and dry-cleaned afterwards. It makes sense, taking this into consideration, to buy a second hand wedding dress. If your budget is tight and you don't mind wearing a dress that has been worn before, go for it. There are a number of sites that sell second hand wedding dresses. Check out the following: sellmyweddingdress.co.uk, preloved.co.uk, bride2bride.co.uk, stillwhite.co.uk and eBay. The sites above sell beautiful designer wedding dresses from designers like Vera Wang (sigh), Caroline Castigliano, Pronovias and Brown's Brides. If you buy from eBay be very wary, ask to see the original receipt, get lots of pictures and check out the feedback of the seller. If they do not have lots of positive feedback: avoid.

On the subject of second hand wedding dresses, **Charity shops** are also a good bet. They always tend to have one or two wedding dresses which will obviously only have been worn once. If you can afford to get it dry cleaned before the big day, even better. If you do get it from a charity shop then make sure you check the dress thoroughly. Check under the armpits and also check for rips and stains. You probably won't be able to return it. To make things easier Oxfam, Red Cross and Barnardo's not only sell second hand dresses but have specialist bridal stores and all of their dresses in store are also listed on their websites. Not all of the dresses are second hand. Some generous designers donate brand new wedding dresses to the store so you really could pick up a bargain while making a difference.

With second hand dresses always factor in dry cleaning costs, alteration costs and delivery charges, all of which can mount up. Try to get an inclusive price.

The High Street: Monsoon, Topshop, H&M, Coast, Ghost and Phase Eight offer some truly beautiful wedding dresses. Their ranges are quite small but they are a lot cheaper than other routes. Monsoon had a very beautiful wedding dress for £200 when I was looking for one. This may be a less unique option however, there might be a lot of other brides buying the same dress as you. This might not matter too much as a lot of white wedding dresses look very similar, you could also style them a completely different way.

Many high street stores also sell beautiful white, bridal-looking dresses that are not wedding dresses but are just as beautiful. Try Next, Lipsy, John Lewis, House of Fraser, French Connection, Reiss, Ted Baker, BHS, Oh My Love, Mango, Zara, Jaeger, Marks And Spencer and L.K Bennett.

If you are pregnant then have your final dress fitting as close to your wedding day as you can get. Some bridal ranges do offer maternity wedding dresses and maternity stores also have evening wear which could be perfect for your wedding dress. An empire line and flowing fabric is the best idea. Although you probably won't show until you are past your first trimester, you might bloat up as this is a common side effect of the first three months of pregnancy. On the other hand, I once saw an episode of Don't Tell The Bride where the bride was heavily pregnant and wore a tight-fitting off-the-shoulder dress, she looked beautiful and stunning. Her bump was out there and proud. I was really struck at how amazing she looked, so do what is right for you. Just make sure there is some stretch in the fabric!

When you buy your wedding dress do not even entertain the idea of vanity sizing. Buy the biggest size and then have your dress fitted. The best way to do this is to choose it according to your biggest measurement: hips, waist, bust etc. The dress will then be fitted in the other areas. Getting married is very stressful and brides tend to lose or gain ten to fifteen pounds. Buying a smaller dress with the intention to exercise and diet into it is also not a very good idea. It is a gamble and you could end up putting your body under too much stress. Many people get ill on their wedding day or miss it altogether, you don't want this to be you because you over-exercised or weren't eating enough. Know your body and how it reacts to stress. This will be an indicator of what size you should buy in case of any eventualities.

When you try on the wedding dresses make sure you can sit down, walk, move around a bit and lift your arms. You are not just going to be standing still all day like a Barbie doll, make sure you can hug your new husband on your wedding day and then dance the night away.

My wedding dress was a kick-walk dress. You had to kick it out and then step. This sounds hard and like you would be walking funny but there is an art to it so you don't look silly! When actress Jennifer Lawrence took a tumble when going to collect her Oscar for Best Actress it was because she was wearing a kick-walk dress but forgot to kick. So keep that in mind. Jennifer Lawrence carried if off, I don't think I could have. (Note: kick-walk dress is not a real term. I made it up but you get the idea)

Watch out for hidden charges when you buy your wedding dress. Ask if there are any additional fees, ask how much fittings cost. Before you pay the deposit find out what happens if you cancel the dress. Do you have to pick it up or will they post it to you? If they post it then how much do they charge? What happens if it goes missing? Get everything in writing and have a good read of their cancellation policy.

Watch out for the salesperson trying to push you to buy a tiara and a veil at the same time as the dress. If you don't know how you are wearing your hair then the veil might not work. If you are anything like me you will also probably be hungry and have been in the store for hours. The store will probably put a veil and tiara on you when you are trying on dresses. They won't put the veil and tiara on every dress, sometimes just the most expensive ones. If you try on one and want to see the full get up then ask them. On the other hand, if you truly fall in love with the veil and tiara then go ahead and buy them. Just make sure it is not an impulse purchase as they are generally very expensive, especially when bought from a bridal store.

On the day of your wedding make sure you wear a strapless dress all day if your dress is strapless. You don't want red marks on your shoulder. Also make sure you wear something loose fitting and that won't ruin your makeup or hair when you have to get changed, like a loose shirt or a strapless dress. Giving your engagement ring a clean is also a good idea. Use an old toothbrush and some washing up liquid and it will look sparkly again in no time at all. Another good tip is to go to the bathroom before you step into your dress. Going to the bathroom in your wedding dress probably won't be easy.

Talking about stepping into a dress: this is the best way to get into your dress. Step into it and pull it up. Then have your bridesmaids do it up at the back and make sure everything looks good. Have your trusty bridesmaids or your makeup artist/hair stylist pin your tiara and veil into place too.

Bolero, Cover up, cape, cloaks, muffs, shawls, shrug.

There are a number of bridal cover up options. Bridal sections of department stores are a good place to start. Debenhams and John Lewis have some good options. Phase Eight has some beautiful bridal wear and Berketex Brides also have some good stuff but can be pricey. They are in House of Fraser and Debenhams. They also have a few standalone stores.

White Or Not?

Not all wedding dresses have to be white and if you have been married before you might not feel like it is appropriate. (Although if Kim Kardashian can wear white on her third wedding day then you can too). White dresses were made popular by Queen Victoria in the nineteenth century as it was the colour debutantes wore at their coming out ball. White is the most popular and traditional choice but you could also get married in ivory. A trend for colourful dresses has gained momentum. In Eastern cultures brides tend to wear red wedding dresses. Pink wedding dresses have been particularly popular in the past few years. Gwen Stefani started the trend when she married Gavin Rossdale in a white and pink John Galliano dress which looked like it was dip-dyed. Kaley Cuoco from The Big Bang Theory got married in an off-the-shoulder bubblegum pink wedding dress. Dita Von Teese got married in a purple dress and Sarah Jessica Parker, AKA Carrie in Sex And The City got married in a black wedding dress. It was very unique but Jessica-Parker later said that she regretted marrying in black so keep in mind that a spontaneous bold choice might carry some weight in the future.

Wedding dresses were white because the bride was supposed to be a virgin but, let's face it, most of us don't marry the first man that we meet and then don't sleep with him until after the wedding. So wear white or don't, just remember that it is your choice and no one else's.

Many Shades of White

If you are having a white dress then it may not seem as simple as you think it is as there are many variations of white. Some will be more flattering than others. Natural white tends to be found in natural fibre, stark white tends to be found in polyester, ivory is a cream shade of white and champagne is off-white and tends to have a soft yellow undertone.

Fittings

If you can get alterations included in the price of your dress then well done. I ended up paying £200 in alteration fees for my dress which was made to measure. In hindsight, paying an extra £200 on top of paying for a bespoke dress to be made for me was actually quite steep. (Or should I say my parents who kindly paid for my dress, thanks Mum and Dad!)

Renting Your Dress

It makes sense to rent a dress that you will only wear once. Many women balk at this though. Either they want to keep their wedding dress for a possible future daughter or just for the sentimentality of it.

There is a growing trend for brides to wear two wedding dresses. An elaborate one for the ceremony and then one that is more practical. You can do this if you want but if you buy a dress that is good enough then you won't need to. You could change your accessories from day to night or hoik your train up. Leaving is another matter however, arriving at your first night hotel wearing your wedding dress will feel great but unless you have a car it is going to be a pain to transport back home. Ditto if you are going on your honeymoon straight away. Get changed just before you head off and give your wedding dress to a trusted member of the wedding party.

Caring For Your Dress After The Wedding

Get it dry cleaned. Even if you are lucky and nothing gets spilt all over it, it will still need freshened up. If it is long, even more so.

A word on dry cleaning

It is very expensive to dry clean a wedding dress. Basically people will just mark everything up because of the sentimental value. Expect to be quoted at least £160 for the dress and £40 plus for the veil. Insane. One dry cleaner even tried to charge me £50 for a box to put it in. Make sure you are not being manipulated due to the sentimental value of your wedding dress. It does not cost £300 to clean a veil and wedding dress and quoting that price is ridiculous. The dry cleaner next to that particular store quoted me £75. Quite a price difference.

Some stains won't show up straight away so you might want to wait until you take your dress to the dry cleaners. When you do take the dress make sure you, or the member of the wedding party who does it for you, points out all of the areas that need attention. Make sure you use a cleaner which specialises in dry cleaning wedding dresses. You don't want to take a risk with something so special and expensive. Ask for recommendations and using a search engine to make sure there are not people giving them negative feedback online is a very good idea. Make sure you inspect the dress carefully, check that the marks and stains are gone but also make sure that no damage has been done. You should specify how you want the dress packed with the cleaner. They will charge you more if you want it boxed but as long as they are not trying to charge you £50 for a piece of cardboard that is fine. The best way to store your wedding dress is wrapped in acid-free tissue paper and then stored in an acid-free box. Don't put anything metal, like your veil if it has a metal clip, in with the dress as it may rust and stain the dress. Make sure the box lets some air in because natural fibres need to be able to breath. If you do not want to store your dress in a box then wrap it in clean white sheets, preferably muslin, in a place that is dry and dark. Check your wedding dress at least every six months to make sure there are no marks or mould setting in. If you store it in your attic it might get too hot and the basement might be too damp. If you have ever lost anything to damp or mould in one of your rooms then do not store your dress there.

What To Do With Your Dress After The Wedding

A couple of years ago there was an awful trend going around where women trashed their wedding dresses. I always hated this as I thought it was incredibly wasteful. I could maybe understand it after a bad divorce but a wedding dress should be a symbol of a beautiful day and all of the love that happened on that day.

If you decide you don't want to keep your dress then there are a number of things you can do. You could have it restyled or dyed into a completely new dress, you could sell it on a number of sites like sellmyweddingdress.co.uk, preloved.co.uk, bride2bride.co.uk, stillwhite.co.uk and eBay. Or you could donate it to charity. The charity option will make you feel good and you will make another woman very happy indeed. Good if you don't need the extra money.

Here is my wedding diary entry on buying my wedding dress:

So I've done it. I have *bought the dress*. Or more accurately, my family bought the dress for me. For which I am eternally grateful as it really helps with the wedding budget.
I live in London and my mother lives in Scotland so I was really panicking about wedding dress shopping. It was something I only wanted to do with my mother but was worried about the logistics. Because of work I only manage to see my family twice a year at most, which is quite painful, about as painful as buying your wedding dress without your mother.

Thankfully fate smiled upon us over New Year and on the 2nd of January we managed to find some wedding dress shops that were open.

The problem is **I hate most wedding dresses.** They are too blingy or too lacy and grown up. Out of all of the dresses in the first store I hated them all and in the second I liked five, three of which turned out to be bridesmaids' dresses (but were white. Really?!). I decided I didn't want an off-the-shoulder dress as at least 80% of wedding dresses I see are off-the-shoulder and although I love that look, I wanted to be different. I am also 'curvy' on top and didn't want to pull my wedding dress up all day, or worry about popping out.

Even though I have been engaged for a while now **nothing prepared me for seeing myself in my wedding dress, that is the moment you finally realise that you are getting married.** "You're getting married", the store-women said. Yes. Yes, I am, I thought. I was so overwhelmed and my mother was welling up. The women in the bridal store also put a tiara and a veil on me to see what it looked like. I never thought I wanted a veil or a tiara but they looked great on and really suited me. I am still not sure what I am doing with my hair for the big day but now I have some ideas.

Both my mother and I loved the first wedding dress I tried on. I tried on the other four and then went back to the first. We called my father and brother to the store and even my father was speechless and had a tear in his eye. Not what you would expect from my dad, he's never quiet. Even my brother, who is very manly, said it was beautiful.

My fiancé was in the vicinity when I bought the dress and I even asked him if he wanted to come and see it. He is very picky and was initially upset when he found out he couldn't see the dress before because of superstition and tradition. He is superstitious so decided against it in the end, although I did catch his face in the mirror when I was in one of the dresses I didn't buy: it was a beautiful moment seeing his smile.

When you go shopping for your wedding dress all of your preconceptions go out of the window. I thought I didn't want lace but my dress has lace. I thought I didn't want a train, but my dress has one. There is even a subtle, elegant amount of bling. I knew I wanted a white dress, I love the **pink dress trend** but it's not for me. When I saw the dress I bought on the hanger I didn't think much of it but something about it grabbed me and I think this is key, you have to try the dress on to make a proper decision.

The other advice I got about buying a wedding dress was to **buy a dress that you can wear again**, therefore making it more economical. I didn't do that either. I bought a wedding dress with a wow factor, it can't be mistaken for anything else.

I thought buying my wedding dress would be much harder, but actually I bought the first wedding dress I tried on. It is being made now and will be ready in three months. Then I will have two fittings. All I have to buy now is the shoes and bouquet. I am so excited. I can't wait until my fiancé sees the dress and we are married. After I bought the dress I said to my fiancé, 'I hope you like it.' and my entire family said 'You will' to him in unison. Let's hope.

The dress was more expensive than I was going to get but every time I look at the pictures my mother took of me in my dress I am overwhelmingly happy.

TK Maxx

TK Maxx is great. Okay everything is last season but that doesn't matter. Fashion and trends change but when something looks good, it looks good. I got my wedding shoes from TK Maxx. They were from Guess and down from hundreds of pounds. I also got a bridal bag from TK Maxx for just £7. They really do have some great finds so have a rummage in the run up to your wedding and see what you can find.

TK Maxx also do wedding dresses. They are last season but, who cares? There will not be a huge range of sizing but you could find a really beautiful dress at a heavy discount.

Underwear

Many brides still wear garters due to the tradition. They hold up your stockings and make for saucy photo opportunities. If you are wearing a streamline dress then make sure the garter doesn't ruin your silhouette.

You might want to wear a slip or petticoat under your dress. It will give a more streamline look and some slips now have slimming technology in them. Make sure it fits properly and is the same shape as your dress. It is also good to have a slip to wear to fittings.

Stockings

Going bare-legged is a good option if you are wearing strappy sandals but otherwise some stockings will make sure your shoes don't rub too much and will hold everything in. If you do want to wear tights with sandals then you could try some footless ones. Footless control stockings are also great. They can even take the strain off your legs after being on your feet all day.

Shapewear

Some spanx can make all of the difference if you are finding it hard to get into your dress. They smooth you out and bring you down about half a dress size. Other shape wear will be just as good. They come in a variety of shapes and sizes for all of the different areas of the body. It might be good to have some on hand for peace of mind.

Wearing The Right Bra

I did not wear the right bra for my initial fitting so I had to pop across the street to Debenhams. Thankfully I managed to make another appointment later that day. The real reason why is because I forgot exactly what the dress looked like. I ordered it in January and by the time it was made and I had my first fitting it was June. Quite a long time. So make a note of what type of underwear you will need on the day. It will save having to re-book a fitting.

If your dress does not have a built in bra you will need one of the following: strapless or spaghetti strap bra or one that is low cut in the back or front. Make sure they are seamless and white or nude. Having some fashion/toupee tape on the day will also be handy if you have to tape anything down or stop anything falling out. You can use it to stop straps falling down too.

Veil or Not

I never thought I would wear a veil but I did. I tried it on with my dress and it looked amazing. The fact that people kept accidentally pulling it on the day was less fun however. It also looked great on the day and really added to the outfit. I clipped it on my hair at the back with a tiara further forward. It was a traditional, almost Princess look I never thought I would go for but I loved it.

When Angelina Jolie married Brad Pitt in August 2014 she wore a silk veil which had been designed by her children. Her six children doodled away and then Donatella Versace embroidered the drawings into the veil. It won't be to everyone's taste but I thought it was beautiful and very unique.

Different Types of Veils

There are a lot of different types of veils. Although they can all look quite similar, the different names are usually so-called because of their length. Here are your options:

Ballerina: Goes all the way to the ankles. Very beautiful and dramatic. **Elbow**: rather obvious: goes to the elbows, **Fingertip**: ditto. One of the most popular veils in the UK, even before the Duchess of Cambridge wore it on her wedding day. **Angel:** doesn't have a specific length but the cut gives it the look of an angels' wings by coming to a point in the back. **Birdcage:** Funnily enough, this was the type of veil I thought I would go for, but I didn't in the end. It stops just below the chin and covers all of the face and is usually attached to a small hat or a fascinator. **Two-tiered:** a veil with more than one layer, comes down to the shoulders. **Blusher:** short and covers the brides face, it is then pushed back over the head. Worn over a longer veil usually. **Chapel:** about seven feet long. **Cathedral:** About ten feet from your headpiece. **Juliet Cap:** very Grace Kelly, worn on your crown and then the veil comes down to your elbows. **Circular:** clipped to the head with a flat comb, can be any length.

Some women don't like the connotations of a veil but if you really want to wear one don't let this stop you. If you look closely at weddings then quite a lot of it is incredibly sexist. Ever noticed that all of the people who traditionally make speeches are male? While a veil's connotations is the handing over of a woman to a man nothing completes a bridal look like wearing a veil and you will feel amazing in one. Let it go and makeup for it by having your maid of honour make a speech.

Some Things To Keep In Mind

If your dress is very bling you might want to wear a plain veil. You don't want to end up looking like a Christmas tree.

Make sure the veil photographs well.

Practice in it. On my wedding day everyone kept pulling my veil. Watch out for that.

The bling on the veil doesn't need to match the dress.

Take your height into consideration. A veil with too much volume might make you look short, also watch out for lines that run across. This will stop the eye and make you look shorter.

You could pick up a bargain along with lots of information on veils at weddingveils-direct.co.uk

Hats, Headpieces, Tiaras

There are other options to a veil, and some that also go with it. Hair jewellery can look stunning and glamorous. Especially with an elaborate up-do.

Some brides wear a hat on their wedding day. My mother wore a hat to her wedding and looked stunningly beautiful. There is a large variety of hats to choose from and they should be less hassle than more fiddly veils and clips. Just make sure you pin the hat on properly and if you end up taking if off at some point, watch out for hat hair. Do it in the bathroom with your bridesmaids so they can restyle your hair and make sure it is not flat. Make sure the hat suits your face, not everyone can carry off a hat. Think about your face shape and what it suits. Some hat options are: large-brimmed hats (not perfect when getting your photo taken, make sure it don't cast a shadow over your face), pillbox, fascinator, cocktail, fedora and trilby.

A headband can also look amazing. I saw a beautiful one by Leo Bancroft for his Tesco (Yes, really) range that had pearls and diamante all along it. There is an endless choice when it comes to headbands. Check eBay and Google Shopping for a good variety.

Here it is **The Tiara**: think about it, how many of us get to be a princess for a day? Yes we are grown women but that doesn't mean we should not live out our fantasies. Not many things look so bridal and it can bring out the girly side of most of us. I never thought I would wear a tiara, I have never been very girly but I did, and I loved it.

Accessories

Accessories can always make an outfit. A special pair of earrings or an heirloom can really add not only to the outfit, but also to the day. A pair of earring from a grandmother who has passed away will make her presence felt in a lovely and sentimental way. Earrings are a very good idea as they catch the light and will be seen at some point even if you wear your hair down. If you are wearing an off-the-shoulder wedding dress then a beautiful necklace can really add a bit of sparkle.

If your wedding dress does not have full length sleeves then a bracelet can really add something. You will, of course, already have a good amount of bling in the shape of your engagement ring and wedding ring so don't over-egg the pudding. Well, unless you want to. It is *your* wedding day.

Gloves

Another option, they particularly work if you are going for a 1950s look.

Jewellery

My mother bought me a beautiful pair of earrings for my wedding day. They were pink sapphire drop earrings. There is a fine lining between wearing some elegant jewellery and looking like a Christmas tree. Your wedding dress should set the tone. If it is very glitzy then you will not need much else but if your wedding dress is simple then you can feel free to bling it up.

Bag

It is handy to have a wedding bag. A clutch will do. Get one of your bridesmaids to hold it during the ceremony.

Shoes

You don't have to get married in a pair of white shoes. I got married in some red high heels and it really made an impact on the day. Guests were taking pictures of my feet all day. Even if your dress is floor length, as mine was, your shoes will still be on show so use this as an excuse to go and buy a new, beautiful pair of shoes.

If your dress is very extravagant you will want your shoes to be quite plain. However, if your dress is quite plain then jazz up those shoes. If you want more height with less pain then heels with a platform will hurt less, as will a pair of wedges. Make sure your shoes are not too small, you don't want to end up crippled on the day. Your feet will also probably expand slightly, especially in hot weather. Make sure they are not too big either, they must either fit perfectly or be a little bit bigger.

I know the temptation to just buy the most amazing shoes but do think about comfort. You will be on your feet all day and you will be thankful later. It is possible – and smart – to pack a pair of flats or just lower-heeled shoes but don't wear those for any official photographs as your dress will be made to fit one pair of shoes, not two different heel heights.

Don't think you have to wear your shoes in the same fabric as your dress, you don't. In fact, it really can mix up your look and add a beautiful detail to have a different colour and fabric.

There are a number of options to jazz up some inexpensive shoes. You could dye them and it won't cost too much. Buy some cheap shoes in satin and then hit the search engines for a cheap but good company that can dye them. Or you can dye them yourself.

You can also buy Blingbacks or some other type of shoe jewellery. These are great as they just clip onto your shoes, either on the front or back.

I also saw a rather brilliant article in a women's magazine where they took a pair of boots, covered them in glue and then put glitter and sequins all over them. The finished result looked amazing and I reckon it would work just as well on a different pair of shoes.

Cheap shoes are not very comfortable usually so just switch to your flats in the evening/after the wedding pictures. In saying that, I have a pair of cheap shoes from Dorothy Perkins that I bought for an audition and I wear them all the time. They are comfortable and still look great.

If you can afford it I would buy the most expensive shoes you can as long as they are not too bridal and you can wear them again. A good, expensive pair of shoes is a great investment piece and you could wear them again and again, all the while knowing that you got married in those shoes.

If you do want to spend a lot of money on a pair of designer shoes then you might want to design your own shoes. It is not a cheap option and would probably cost in the region of £300 but, if you were buying a pair of expensive shoes anyway, having some made to fit your feet and style exactly will be worth the money. At least they will be comfortable. You could even get your wedding date inscribed on the shoes and you even get a pair that is entirely bespoke. Upper Street are a company that do this and so do shoesofprey.com

Comfort

Same ballet pumps in your bridal bag will probably save your life on your wedding day. Some flat, or lower-heeled shoes will really help when you have been on your feet all day. They really will give that 'ah' feeling. The other option is that you kick off your heels and dance the night away in your bare feet.

For extra comfort you can buy padded shoe inserts. There are a number of options for these. You can buy inserts for the back of the shoe to stop rubbing or blisters, there are gel pads that you put under the ball of your foot to ease burning and you can also buy a blister stick which you can rub onto your toes and the back of your heels to stop excess rubbing. Vaseline will also have the same effect.

I have heard of some women rubbing the bottom of their feet with alcohol to numb the feet. Some people swear by it.

It is also very important to wear your shoes in before the wedding day. Do this on a clean floor or a rug. Practise dancing in them too. You might also want to rough up the soles with a knife so the shoes are not too smooth and have a bit of grip. This will stop you falling over.

THE GROOM'S OUTFIT

Just like women, men should dress to suit their body shape. Think about what suits you when choosing your groom's outfit. Most grooms rent their outfit but not all. Some get a bespoke suit made, others buy one off the shelf. There are a lot of options however.

The groom buys his outfit with his best man or/and the rest of his wedding posse like his ushers and friends. There are no rules or superstitions about a bride seeing the groom's outfit before the wedding so you could buy his outfit with him or even see it beforehand. You may want to talk about colour schemes with your bride-to-be. If she is wearing ivory then you might want to wear an ivory shirt. You may also want your tie or handkerchief to match the wedding colours. You don't have to co-ordinate of course, only if you want. It is too 'matchy' for some people.

One thing to keep in mind is the weather. I still feel slightly guilty about asking a few of my friends and my father to wear a kilt to my wedding. They were sweltering in the July heat but they looked amazing so it was worth it in the end. If you are getting married in the summer you might want to avoid a heavy wool suit and opt for some linen instead.

The best man and groom should be dressed in a similar fashion. They don't have to match but they should not clash. If one is wearing a morning suit, then the other should as well. Ushers should also either look similar or have something of note that is the same. Like a waistcoat, handkerchief or a tie.

Kilts

If you are Scottish you can go for the kilt option. Kilts look amazing and the full Scottish regalia is something to behold. Proper Highland dress with the kilt, sporran and waistcoat looks brilliant. It looks great in pictures too. Wear your own tartan if you have some, if not then choose one you have a special connection with or one that really grabs you. My dad has an English surname despite being a Scot and he wore a gorgeous black and white kilt. My best man, Steve McAleavy, is also Scottish but his surname is Irish so he wore a family tartan that was equally beautiful.

Military Uniform

Only an option if you are actually in the military but it looks amazing. Women love a man in uniform. Richard Gere in An Officer And A Gentleman springs to mind.

Suits

Make sure the suit fits. If you are not buying a new one, get it tailored and even if you do buy a new one off the shelf, unless it fits perfectly, have it tailored. If you are getting a suit made make sure you give it enough time. At least three months.

Tuxedos

Ditto for tuxedos. You obviously won't be able to get it tailored if it is rented but do make sure it fits well.

Dinner suit

You can wear a black, white or ivory dinner jacket. White and ivory work well in summer. White or ivory can still be worn with black trousers.

Formal suit

This is not only a good look for a wedding but can also be a great investment buy. A three-piece suit can be worn many times over. If you can afford to get one made, do so. Good colours include navy, beige, black, pale grey and white. You can even get a patterned suit for a very unique look. Generally worn with a tie or a cravat, this is a very popular choice.

Morning Suit

My husband wore a morning suit to our wedding and I do have to say, he looked incredibly handsome. The morning coat is a very formal choice but don't let that put you off. Weddings are formal and the groom is supposed to stand out. Coats are black or grey and so are trousers. You can mix and match the colours of the coat and trousers. Morning coats are worn with a tie or cravat.

Tails

Tails are a jacket that is short in the front and long in the back, it has two longer tails which hang down the back. This is a very formal option. Usually worn with a bow tie and a formal, white shirt.

Tuxedo or Black tie

A popular option in America. For formal weddings. Looks great on. Black, grey or navy are all colour options. A tuxedo is worn with a bow tie, waistcoat, cummerbund and braces. Wear the cummerbund or the waistcoat but not both. Trousers are usually flat fronted or have one pleat. Has the added benefit of making people look like James Bond. It is easy to stamp your own personality onto a tuxedo as there are so many different ways to wear it.

Lounge suit

Good for an informal wedding. You could get the suit and jacket made from different material. Looks smart but is more informal.

There are a few different **shirt options** and you should go with the one that not only suits your outfit, but also you. For **collar style** you can go for **mandarin**, which is a collar that does not fold over and is high-necked, **spread**, which is the most popular one and is the same size all around and **wing**, which is winged at the front.

For **neckwear**: a bow tie, cravat or tie are all an option. Each can look great, just make sure it matches the outfit.

A handkerchief can look very smart and could be in one of the wedding colours. Gives an extra something.

Other Details

Cufflinks are a great look. It is the little details like this that really lift an outfit. Try for some personalised cufflinks or some which have a sentimental meaning, a gift from your future wife perhaps. My parents bought my husband some beautiful cufflinks that said 'groom' on them and my father wore ones that said 'father of the bride'. They were really lovely and added a beautiful personal touch to the day.

Waistcoat

Men look very dashing in waistcoats and one that is silk, colourful or extravagant can ensure the groom stands out. All of the male wedding party can wear waist-coats but the groom's must be different as he must stand out and not 'blend in' amongst the ushers and best man. Make sure that your waistcoat covers the top of the waistband. Waistcoats are also great for making men look slimmer. They give a streamlined look.

Shoes

If you buy new shoes then make sure you wear them in a little by wearing them around the house. You don't want sore feet on the day. Make sure your shoes are in good condition. Check them for scuffs, make sure the shoelaces match and are in good condition and check the heel is not worn.

There are no general rules on men's wedding shoes but a pair of black oxfords will always look good (full confession, my husband's choice of shoe on our wedding day). You could wear colourful shoes or even colourful socks. Just make sure you take the label off the bottom if they are new and that they match your outfit.

Renting Versus Buying

The renting versus buying debate may be decided on financial factors. If you are wearing a suit to your wedding then getting one made would be a great investment that would pay off in the end. However, if you wore a tuxedo or a morning suit then you probably would not get as much wear out of it. Another thing to factor into your decision is that you will be looking at these pictures for the rest of your life. Looking good on your wedding day is just as important for a man as it is for a woman.

It is possible to rent and still look good but just make sure you get there early if you are getting married in peak wedding season, you don't want to have to pick from whatever is left. If you are going on your honeymoon straight away then have a member of the wedding party return the outfit for you in time. When you pick your wedding outfit up check that it is in good condition and that it has no stains and nothing is missing.

Men tend to rent their outfits but women can rent dresses too. This obviously makes financial sense. You only wear the dress once and it costs a considerable amount of money. Despite this, many women hate the thought of not owning their wedding dress. The sentimental value is not to be underestimated.

Shoes - Women

Don't feel like you have to get married in a traditional pair of wedding shoes. They don't need to be made out of fabric, or white or Ivory. I got married in a pair of red high heels with blue 'I Do' stickers on the bottom. The guests loved them and everyone kept photographing them. It was something bold and unique. The rest of my wedding look was quite traditional so I wanted to rebel with my shoes.

Where To Find Your Outfit

Bridal magazine will have a lot of resources, yes, even for men. Moss Bros is popular and have lots of stores all over the UK. The Moss Bros in London is in Covent Garden. Wedding blogs and websites will also have plenty of shop and tailor recommendations. Search engines are obviously going to be your secret weapon. In fact, it should not be hard to find anything in this day and age. Make sure where you get your outfit is easy to get to however, you will need to pick it up a few days before the wedding and you (or someone else if you are on honeymoon) will have to drop it off. It is best to keep things local.

It is a good idea for all of the male wedding party to go clothes shopping together. That way you can negotiate for a bulk deal. Sometimes you can get the groom's wedding outfit for free or at a discount.

There are also some sites on the internet where you can buy bespoke suits for a very cheap price. You measure yourself and then the suit is made overseas. I would give it plenty of time if you are choosing this option. Try www.asuitthatfits.com

When renting make sure you know what is included in the price.

A Word On Grooming

Make sure the wedding party shave, have a haircut and look clean and tidy. Grooming will be remembered. Dirty fingernails are not a good look.

BRIDESMAIDS, FLOWER GIRLS AND PAGE BOYS

Choosing Bridesmaids' Dresses

Gone are the days when a variety of women of different ages and sizes had to wear the same awful dress. The best thing to do these days is choose a colour and then have the bridesmaids wear beautiful dresses that suit them and their shape. I chose navy blue for my bridesmaids and one of my regrets of my wedding planning is not having all of my maids together and going shopping for dresses.

You can ask your bridesmaids to buy their own dresses but if you are doing this then definitely just give them a colour, don't ask them to buy a horrible dress they will never wear again. Also, make sure you buy them a present if they buy their own dress. It is only fair. Remember that your friends are not made of money, and even if they are rich, no one wants to be taken advantage of.

Decide if you want your bridesmaids to look like individuals or like a traditional wedding party. The first decision is: do you want them to look very individual or to wear the same dress? Or different dresses in the same fabric and colour? If you really do want them all in the same dress then make sure it will suit everyone's different body shape. If one of your bridesmaids is pregnant you might want to take her shopping first as it might be hard to find her a dress. Go for an empire line and loose fabrics. Flowing material will work and don't put her in stilettos either. A thick heel or wedge will be needed.

You can buy beautiful bridesmaids dresses on the high street. Little Mistress, Topshop, Dorothy Perkins and H&M all have affordable dresses with a wow factor. If you want to shell out and have a fun day then sites like maidstomeasure.com give you and your bridesmaids the opportunity to design your own dresses either online or over champagne in its store. It will cost between £215-255. They will look very wow indeed. Oh, and talking about the wow factor, make sure your maids look amazing on the day. Only insecure women try and make their bridesmaids look ugly. If you are getting your makeup done, you could get your bridesmaids' makeup done too. This is an extra nice treat if they are paying for their own dresses.

If you want to make a day of it you could go to an outlet village like Bicester near Oxford. Kate Middleton has been known to shop there and you could have a day out and then pick up a bargain. They have Jigsaw, Donna Karen and Prada.

For flower girls or younger bridesmaids: many brides dress them in a white or cream dress and then add a sash in the colour of the older bridesmaids' dresses. You might want to include a cardigan or something to keep the kids warm.

Page boys' outfits should be easy to find. Don't buy them too far in advance because children tend to have growth spurts. A shirt and trousers will work and you could add a tie in the wedding colours. Suits are super cute on younger children and you don't have to spend a fortune. You can even get them from supermarkets like George at Asda, it doesn't make much sense to spend a lot when they will only grow out of them and get them dirty.

Mother of The Bride

It is a good idea to coordinate with the mothers of the groom and bride to make sure they don't wear the same outfit. Or the same colour. Traditionally the bride's mother chooses the style and colour of her outfit and then lets the groom's mother know. The idea being that the groom's mother then chooses something similar in terms of formality and won't wear colours that clash. They should not dress the same obviously. As long as it does not clash let your mother wear what she wants. She will feel more comfortable if what she is wearing suits her and her personality.

If she needs to wear a hat then she shouldn't wear one which is wider than her shoulders and if your mother is petite then make sure she does not wear a hat that overwhelms her. If she is not petite then she shouldn't wear one that is too small. She could also wear a fascinator or a jewelled clip. Keep in mind that she will be photographed a lot so make sure the hat does not cast too much of a shadow and that you can see her face clearly. She will want to be seen on her daughter's wedding day.

Dads

Dads should dress to suit the wedding party. Wearing something similar to the ushers would be a good idea. Dads could join the wedding party when they are buying the groom's outfit. If not, they should be told what the groom and best man are wearing. Dads should not dress like the groom or best man. The groom is supposed to stand out and look different from everyone else. The best man too but less so.

CHAPTER 10: BEAUTY

Never in your life will you feel more like a film star than on your wedding day. You will feel like a VIP and everything will be about you. Enjoy every minute of this, you deserve it and it will also probably never happen again. Although booking beauty treatments and hiring a makeup artist and hair stylist is a very good idea if you can afford it try not to go overboard. You want your groom to recognise you when you walk down the aisle. There is even a trend for brides to have cosmetic surgery and non-invasive treatments like botox and collagen injections before the big day. While there is nothing wrong with making your own choices in regards to surgery and other non-invasive beauty treatments, be careful as you may be acting out of character. You want to look like yourself on your wedding day and getting something permanent during the run up to a wedding, when stress and tension is high, could turn out to be a mistake. In the 9th-16th 2014 edition of Grazia magazine there was a statistic that said that 40% of men think women wear too much makeup and look better without it. You might want to turn it up for your wedding pictures but don't do anything out of character.

There has been a recent trend for brides not to wear makeup on their wedding day. I love the pictures of these weddings and think the brides look amazing. I wouldn't be brave enough to do it myself but they look beautiful and confident. A number of brides are also walking down the aisle wearing glasses. This is another trend that I love. They looked stunning.

In saying all of this: if you want to wear a lot of makeup then do. My makeup look for my wedding was quite strong but that was mostly because I didn't look in a mirror before I left the house. In hindsight, I am happy about that. I looked like a more extreme version of myself but it worked. My husband thought I was wearing too much makeup, of course, and thought I looked better without it, but it looked good on camera and gave me confidence that I looked good despite only having had a few hours' sleep.

In the run up to your wedding day exercising three times a week at least, drinking lots of water, eating well: all of those clichéd things will really pay off. Even if you don't want to lose weight, working out improves your skin and makes you look healthier. I was on a bridal boot camp in the run up to my wedding. I exfoliated regularly, used a face mask once a week and made sure I moisturised regularly. It all paid off and made a difference. I would recommend the same to anyone else. If you really want to step it up a notch, smoothies and eating lots of vegetables will leave you glowing. As will cutting out alcohol and sugar. I cut down drastically on sugar in the run up to my wedding and barely drank alcohol. Although the sugar is now back in my diet this really made a difference to my skin and how I looked on the day. I didn't diet as I never have in my life, but I tried to be as healthy as possible.

Stress is detrimental to both health and beauty. While it is impossible not to stress out in the run up to a wedding try to stay as calm as possible. Do deep breathing or even meditation if that is your thing. Even going for a walk can put things into perspective.

If you can afford it start having facials three months before your wedding. Don't start just before as your skin will break out and might not calm down before the big day. A good investment you won't regret is a good spot treatment. Alternatively buy some aspirin and if you get a spot, crush half an aspirin and then add a tiny bit of water to make it into a paste, put on the skin for a little while and then wipe off. This is cheaper and far more effective than most spot treatments. I review beauty products all of the time and that trumps any spot treatment I have tried.

Another great beauty treatment to have if you can afford it is a massage. I had a full body massage at one of the posh hotels in London and afterwards I felt amazing. Great for relaxing you and sorting out any tired and aching muscles.

Beauty counters in department stores will have beauty consultants who can offer lots of great advice. They will want you to buy something obviously but you don't have to. If you are feeling pressure then say you want to think about it and will come back and buy the product at some other point. Investing in good skincare, especially in the run up to your wedding, will pay off in the long run so don't be scared to treat yourself.

Wedding Makeup

When Kate Middleton married Prince William and became a Duchess she did her own makeup. It started a trend and now many women do their own makeup. Some beauty counters in department stores also give free wedding makeup lessons. Bobbi Brown give an hour long lesson. Then if you buy something over £60 you get a free wedding makeup gift set.

If you are incredibly good at doing your own makeup then go for it. If you are anything less than perfect then I would hire a makeup artist. You are going to be photographed and filmed, makeup that looks good on camera is very different from makeup that looks good in real life. I had my makeup done by a wonderful makeup artist called Kay Cunningham and it was one of my top wedding decisions. In the two nights running up to my wedding I had a maximum of four hours sleep. In forty-eight hours. Yup. Brutal. On my wedding day *no one could tell*. What's more, in the pictures and wedding film I look good. All thanks to the wonderful power of makeup and a professional doing what they do best.

This is not an area where I would skimp. Hire a professional. You will look at your wedding photos for the rest of your life and so will your grandchildren. Make sure you look your best on the day.

If you are going to tan for your wedding then make sure it doesn't transfer onto your dress. Having a professional spray tan three days before will look natural and will not ruin your beautiful dress.

Hiring a professional makeup artist is a very stressful business. There are a lot of wedding makeup artists out there and choosing just one can be hard indeed. This will be even harder on a limited budget. Be honest about your budget and see if you can negotiate on cost. You might not be able to because a lot of makeup artists are in high demand. If you are having a weekday wedding, or you book last minute and the makeup artist is not doing anything else on that day then you could get a good deal. It will be harder if you are marrying in July on a weekend. Always try and get some money off however, maybe they could do a bridesmaid for free? Asking for a package deal is always a good idea.

If you have a specific makeup artist in mind and they are popular, then make sure you book them months in advance. A makeup trial will cost between £50-80 for the bride and then either the same or a little less for a bridesmaid or the mother of the bride. The actual price of getting your makeup done on the day is usually upwards of £130 for the bride and then a little less for each member of the bridal party. No, it certainly is not cheap but it will be less if you don't live in London or are not getting married there. Although a makeup artist having to travel to the middle of nowhere will add that on to the bill. They will charge travel expenses.

Ask for recommendations when choosing a makeup artist. Make sure they are fast and won't make you late to your own wedding and always ask to see lots of pictures of their bridal work. Not just their normal makeup portfolio, bridal makeup is different. Remember that your makeup will have to last for ten-to-twelve hours. They need to know what they are doing.

Make sure you get along with your makeup artist. You will spend a good few hours with them and they will be the last person you spend your time with just before you step into your dress and you want to be centred and calm.

If you are low on pennies but really want your makeup done professionally then you could get a student from a local beauty college to do your makeup and hair. They probably won't charge much and even less if you let them use your pictures for their portfolio. Just make sure they are good and reliable and have a look at their work first. If you don't mind getting up early on your wedding day you could also book an appointment in a department store at one of the beauty counters. They will do your makeup for free. Try MAC, Benefit or Bobbi Brown.

Have one of your bridesmaids on beauty look out on your wedding day. Have them make sure your makeup and hair is in place and, if not, are on hand to fix the problem.

Long lasting makeup to last your entire wedding day.

A lot of brides go for a subtle look, and this does look great and very bridal. Just make sure you are wearing enough makeup for the camera. Also make sure you are not pressured into a look that you don't want. If you want to wear bright red lipstick on your wedding day, do it.

I interviewed my wedding makeup artist, Kay Cunningham, she did a good job on the day as I actually looked like I had had more than three hours sleep.

Here is her biography:

My first passion was fashion, growing up around both parents making custom made clothing for the community. Thirteen years ago I discovered another passion as I studied Art & Fashion Design. As makeup is a part of the artistic world it made sense when I started, I just adapted to it. I have worked for the best of luxury cosmetic brands such as Versace Makeup, Guerlain Cosmetics, Presciptives and Trish McEvoy. I have also done work for Chanel, YSL and Givenchy.

In late December 2012 I decided to become a freelance makeup artist after a second redundancy. It was a tough decision but it has made me stronger going through the challenges and developing my portfolio along the way. Bridal makeup has always been one of my favourite kinds of makeup to do as I'm making a bride up on probably the most important day of her life. I get excited doing a bride and hoping to get a smile after! I also work on other projects like films, editorial, fashion, fashion shows and events. I also have some lovely private clients I've met along the way and some are now good friends. If there was one company I could go back to work for it is Trish McEvoy.

Tell us about your experience as a Makeup Artist.

My experience as a makeup artist varies from working for luxury cosmetics brands to doing film projects, creative photo shoots, music videos, demos, makeovers at the studio, events, private clients and bridal makeup. I enjoy every project, there is never a dull moment and I get to meet so many lovely clients along the way.

Do you think hiring a Makeup Artist on your wedding day is important?

Absolutely! It might be the most important day of your life. You want to look flawless and that way you are not pressuring any of your friends by saying they can do it.

What kind of looks do you recommend?

If it is a traditional wedding ceremony you can keep a natural look for eye makeup with pastel shades, along with gold. For the lips, I love to see a bride in a rosy or nude lip colour. Some brides love it fierce but your wedding day is not over at the ceremony, a lot of brides change their makeup for the reception, some brides prefer to keep the same look throughout the day.

What if the bride is unsure of what look she wants?

A bridal trial is strongly advised before the wedding day. That way the makeup artist can make suggestions, social media is also useful for makeup ideas with an inspiring creative makeup artist.

What things should a bride take into consideration when she is making decisions on her wedding makeup?

Think of how you would love your soon-to-be husband to remember you after the wedding day, after the trial you can share the images and if he gives a thumbs up, you are good to go!

Do you have any tips for brides who want to do their own makeup?

No DIY please, book a bridal makeup artist, and to avoid a rush it's better to book way in advance. It's important as your face will be the most looked at, apart from you wedding dress!

What is your favourite wedding look?

My favourite is the natural flawless look with gold or natural eye shadows, rose or nude lip colour and highlights with a bit of soft blush.

What are your top beauty tips?

There are too many, here are some for brides or any female.

1. When doing your makeup for an occasion (medium to full makeup) Start with your eyes, then foundation and concealer etc., that way you won't need to clean the eye shadow dust off your under eye, saves a lot of time.
2. Ever wonder why your makeup slips off your face after 3 hours? The reason is due to how you dress your face, for longer lasting use a face and eye primer, that way it will keep your foundation and eye shadow intact especially for normal or oily skin tone.
3. For a fuller coverage you can build up a medium foundation (liquid) by applying it first with a brush then again after applying concealer to the main areas needed on your face (depends on your skins condition) followed by your choice of powder (I prefer compress powder for going out)
4. Do not wear a darker foundation for a tan effect, I always tell my clients that and stick with a perfect match, then add bronzing powder or contouring shades to compliment and create contour effect. If you are unsure please pop along to your favourite beauty brand for consultation.

5. After applying lipstick add lip liner for defining the lip shape. If you have small lips apply on the lip line for a fuller effect, for medium or full lips apply liner on the inner lip line and remember that anyone can wear a red lipstick by choosing the correct one for your skin tone

What are your favourite products to use on brides?

Anything luxurious and of good quality!

What about hair? Any tips for great bridal hair?

Most brides tend to want pin up styles but remember there are a lot of different face shapes to consider. Flattering curls are also a lovely choice. Extensions will bring more volume. Book an appointment at your hair stylist about five days before the wedding if adding extensions.

How does a bride stop her makeup running or sliding off her face?

It depends on a lot of things. If in summer avoid hot rooms, but if the makeup artist dresses the bride's face correctly the only thing that might need topping up is your T-Zone and lipstick.

What waterproof makeup do you recommend?

Mascara and eye liner pencil (Read the benefit of each product before purchasing).

Any other top beauty and makeup tips?

If you have been using the same skin care for the past 2- 5 years and it is not doing what it says, I suggest you change it because it won't get any better for your skin.

Thank you, Kay

So there you go. Advice from a professional.

Hair

You might be comfortable doing your hair yourself. Or having a blow-dry at a salon the day before so it looks its best. You could also go to your hairdresser in the morning. Otherwise hiring a hair stylist for a wedding can cost upwards from £120. It will depend on how you want to style your hair. It could be less for a weekday wedding. You could also go the beauty college route again if you are trying to save money. Many salons also do lessons on how to do your hair. These range from fish-tails to blow-drys. Take a bridesmaid with you to help on the day. The knowledge is something you can use again and again so it will be worth the money. For a budget version there are a ton of beauty bloggers out there and most of them have You

Tube channels where they teach you how to do amazing things with your hair. With some practice, and a good deal of patience, you could have a wonderful hair style which you do all by yourself. John Frieda's salon also has a YouTube channel which has plenty of great how-to clips on how to achieve the perfect hair style of your choice. You may want to wash your hair the day before your wedding so it is less slippery if you are having an up do. If your hair looks very 'done' at the beginning of the day, don't worry. It has to last for about ten hours and will probably become more relaxed during the day.

The most important thing is to choose a hairstyle that suits you and your face shape. You want to look amazing but you also want to feel comfortable.

Allow enough time to get your hair done on the day and make sure you don't go last, it will be stressful and you will either be late to your own wedding or only half-done. Keep in mind that if you are having a hair stylist come to you they will charge you for the travel. This can add up if you are getting married far away from their location. Going to the salon is cheaper if that is possible or hiring a trainee stylist. If you are trying something very different, a new hair colour or highlights then make sure you allow plenty of time before the big day in case you don't suit something or it goes wrong.

Make sure your hair looks good from the back. Your guests will spend a lot of time looking at the back of your head.

For your wedding day it is worth investing in some extensions if you want your hair to look fuller. You can get clip in ones or bespoke ones that will be your exact hair colour. If you want a beautiful, full head of hair then go for it. We could all do with a little oomph sometimes. I still feel like I should have gotten some extensions for my hair on my wedding day.

Timings

You make think that the bride should go first but if she is waiting for hours then her makeup won't look fresh. It is very important she is done on time of course but one of the bridesmaids should go first. Then the bride. Anyone else should go after that but the bride should have her makeup refreshed before she leaves to go to the venue. Also make sure you have powder and the lipstick you have used in your bridal bag.

Bridal Boot Camp

I set a target weight to reach for my wedding day so I wouldn't get too thin. (Yes, there is such a thing). Unfortunately I then got a tummy bug and a throat infection in the week running up to my wedding and lost another half a stone. I was pretty annoyed to be honest but it turned out to be a good thing because I found out – on my wedding day (!) – I was pregnant and, although my waist and hips were fine, my breasts had already started to grow. It took my maid of honour, Paloma, and my bridesmaid, Holly, to zip the dress all the way past my bosom whilst they both chimed, 'It's okay, it's just because it is a hot summer's day, you are just swollen.' Yup, that is why they are amazing and I chose them as my maids.

To be honest, pre-wedding I was a size 10/12 and there is absolutely nothing wrong with being a size 10/12. I am, however, only 5.5" and as someone who is also an actor I know that the camera adds 10 pounds. At least. Too many brides go overboard but it is a good idea to go on a health kick, even if you don't want to lose weight. On the other hand, if you do want to lose some weight be firm and polite with people who make rude comments about it. It is your body and as long as you are not starving yourself or over-exercising then you can do whatever you want. Some people have a problem when other people lose weight and thin-bashing is a real thing.

It is best to keep in mind that you want to look like you on your wedding day. The best version of yourself, but still you. I find the trend for women having cosmetic surgery for their wedding baffling. Surely your groom wants to marry the person he proposed to, not someone he doesn't even recognise as they walk up the aisle?

For bridal boot camp it is best to eat as healthily as possible. I cut down on sugar and caffeine. I drank plenty of water and made sure I had my five-a-day in fruit and vegetables. I also took a multivitamin and Omega 3. In the weeks running up to the wedding I also started taking probiotics as they sort the bacteria in your tummy out and help make it flat. I went for plenty of walks and got some fresh air. Here are some more tips for looking your best:

Use a weekly face mask.
If you can afford it, have a facial.
Have a manicure and pedicure the week before the wedding.
Use a hair mask.
Up your water intake. Dehydration makes everyone look awful.
Get your hair trimmed/cut just before the wedding. It will look much better.
Exfoliate and moisturise as much as you can. It will make your skin glow on the day.
Don't be bullied into tanning but, if you do, be careful and don't do it the night before. Fake tan + white dress is not a good combination.
Use a highlighter on the day across your cheekbones, under your eyebrows on the outer edge and on the cupid bow of your mouth.
Have your teeth whitened. Either at home or professionally. It will make a huge difference to the wedding photos.

CHAPTER 11: RECEPTION

Your wedding reception can be a bit nerve-racking. Especially if you are not used to being the centre of attention. Everyone will want to talk to you and it will just be sinking in that you are now man and wife. But before we get to this part there is the planning and here is my first piece of advice: relax. It will all be okay, it really will.

Once you have your venue planning your reception will get easier. You will know the space you have to work with and you should also know the rough amount of guests that will be attending. So now you can get creative and add personal touches that will make your wedding day memorable to your guests. Look in bridal magazines, blogs and Pinterest for some ideas and start putting the feel of your wedding together. Ask the venue if there are any restrictions on decoration and then go for it. You could ask the venue manager what works with the venue and what other couples have done but make sure they don't try to push you into doing something you don't want to do. This is about the personal style of you and your groom to be. Another thing to check with the venue is what they supply and what they don't. It is better to get a clear view from the start so you know what you are dealing with. Check out how long the venue takes to set up and break things down. If their seats are grubby then think about hiring some seat covers. Also check if the venue has other events that day. Enquire if you have to use the venue's suppliers. They might not be to your style. Some venues will charge you extra if you do not go with their suppliers so watch out for this. If you don't like something in the venue ask if it can be removed for the day. Another thing to ask is where the top table should go and if there is any air-conditioning or heating.

If your venue has a drive lighting it with candles is a good touch. As is waiters with drinks at the entrance. A guest book is not only a wonderful personal touch, giving guest a chance to express their happiness for you both, but also something that you can keep for years to come.

Not many guests bring their gift to the actual wedding anymore but it is still a good idea to have a table somewhere where guests can put their cards, presents and sign the guestbook. This is also a good place to put the seating plan. A basket is also a good idea and makes it easier to transport the contents. A box or an old suitcase would work just as well and would be even better if you could decorate it. Make sure you get a trusted wedding party member to take the box/basket at the end of the night. It goes without saying but don't open your cards or wedding presents at the reception, it isn't appropriate.

Getting a member of the wedding party to encourage people to leave personal message in the guestbook is a good idea. I asked my husband's best man to mention it in his speech and my amazing maid of honour, Paloma, also hounded people for me. We love our guestbook and the messages inside it mean so much to us. Guestbooks don't have to be expensive. Many stationery stores sell them but you could also buy a good hardback notebook or buy a cheap one online.

Lighting is very important. Try to visit your venue at the same time you will be having your wedding. Knowing what the lighting will be like lets you know what needs done. Discuss lighting with the venue. Do they supply candles? Do they change the lighting throughout the day? Will they dim the lights during the first dance?

If you want props like candelabras and vases but don't want to buy them then you could rent them from a prop shop or an antique shop. Just make sure you have someone return the items so you don't run up any extra fees and make sure that renting is not more expensive than buying. Remember that you can sell anything you don't want after your wedding on eBid or eBay.

It is possible that you will get very excited about the reception and doing things for it but do remember it is a wedding. The best way to decorate your venue is with flowers and candles. You should not feel pressured to do anything else unless you want to. As long as there is some music, nice flowers, some candles and food and drink then your guests can entertain themselves and will happily do so. If you want to add honeycombs, balloons and magicians to your wedding do so, but don't feel you have to spend every second entertaining your guests. They will probably be happy to just mingle and then dance later.

Drinks Reception

If you do not want people boozing too early then you can start them off with some tea and coffee, along with some water and sparkling elderflower. We did this as we wanted to pace our guests. Although we did see some guests with beer and wine which made me feel like a bad hostess. I didn't expect them to go to the bar but I guess they didn't realise the wine would be flowing so soon after. We also had tea and coffee after the meal as it is a great digestive and people will probably appreciate it after they have had so much wine during the wedding breakfast. It also felt very civilised.

Welcoming Guests

A receiving line, where the bride and groom used to receive certain members of the wedding party, is a bit outdated but you can still do it if you want. If you are having a big wedding you might want to cut the receiving line down to a certain number of key wedding people: mother-of-the-bride, mother-of-the-groom etc. Although these people you will already have seen on a regular basis anyway. Receiving lines are a bit outdated now so you can forgo them and then make your rounds at the reception.

You may want a master of ceremonies if the venue does not already supply one. You could have a family member do it or allocate certain times to the best man, maid of honour and ushers if you would like. If you have a small wedding it will be easier to keep things in check but if not, a master of ceremonies will make sure everything runs on time and let people know what is happening. If you don't have a member of the wedding party or a family member making sure things run on time then the cost of a master of ceremonies may be worth it. They will help things run smoothly and also ensure that things run on time. Make sure that anyone given the task will be organised and hold off on the drinking. Give them all of the details they will need and buy them a present after.

CHAPTER 12: FLOWERS

Flowers really add to a wedding. In fact, the only decorations that you really need are flowers and candles. Everything else is extra. Not that there is anything wrong with extra.

When choosing your flowers try to choose them in season. Your florist should be able to help you find your way. I found it quite hard to find the names of flowers that I liked on the internet. There is a magazine called Wedding Flowers which might be worth buying to help you get a clear idea of what you have in mind.

Flowers are the main decoration feature during a wedding so getting them right is important. That does not mean you have to spend a lot of money or have something formal. Your flowers should reflect your personality and the style of your wedding. To gain inspiration type 'flowers' or 'bridal bouquets' into a search engine then click the image tab. Magazines, blogs and Pinterest are also great sources for inspiration. Rock N Roll Bride will also have lots of pictures of real life weddings you can gain inspiration from. Tear pictures out of magazines and save images to your computer or tablet. You can share these with your florist later who can then advise on whether that flower is in season or would work.

My florist was very helpful. I knew I wanted roses and wanted some blue flowers. I wanted the flowers to match our colour scheme so I had pale pink and white roses, some blue bee and foliage. They looked great on the day. Choosing flowers according to your colour scheme is a good idea but you don't have to. They can be anything at all.

Upon the shock of receiving a quote for your flowers, yes, unfortunately they are usually that expensive, you will wonder why they cost so much. Surely you could even just go and pick your own flowers. Unfortunately you cannot just go and pick flowers yourself. Under the Wildlife and Countryside Act 1981 you cannot uproot any wild plant without permission from the landowner/occupier. Breaking the law just before your wedding is probably not a good idea. You could grow some flowers yourself however, or you might have a friend or relative with some beautiful flowers growing in their garden.

Here was the breakdown I got from my florist. I haven't changed anything.

Bridal posy £55
white roses avalanche three stems
pink roses sweet avalanche three stems
blue bee three stems
foliage Rosemarie eucalyptus dark pistachio

4 bridesmaids' posies   each £25
pink roses sweet avalanche one stem
White Rose avalanche two stems

blue bee two stems
mixed foliage

4 buttonholes each £4.75
white roses avalanche

Four tables   each £23
seven jam jars arrangements
pink phlox three stems
alstroemeria white three stems
blue bee three stems
mixed foliage

White orchid plant £30
white container £4.75
delivery £12

Total £381.75

Finding a Florist

My main tip is to find a florist near you! We live in London and do not have a car so I had to carry eight vases on a bus all the way to Kingston. There was a little bit of walking in each direction and it certainly was not fun, especially as it was July and one of the hottest days of the year.

Secondly, make sure you don't get screwed over on the price. I mean, really, how much can flowers cost? The answer is, because of the 'W' bomb: a significant amount. Hundreds.

Get recommendations when you start looking for a florist. Make sure they are reliable, professional and good at their job. Ask the editors of local bridal magazines, wedding bloggers, the venue, other wedding suppliers and friends for recommendations. A Twitter or Facebook plea for advice and recommendations could also bring up some good possibilities. Make sure the florist's style is the same as yours, take a look at their website and make sure it looks professional and is up to date. Check if they are on social media. The internet is your friend, use it. Meet possible florists in person to make sure you get along with them and to get a quotation based on your ideas. Don't feel like you have to go with the first person you see, shop around. Ask to see photographs of previous wedding that they have done. If the florist has worked with your venue before this is certainly a bonus. If they will provide vases or containers this is also a huge bonus. Even if they charge extra for these. Asking them if you could possibly rent any vases or extras is also worth doing. They might say yes and it will save you time and money. Do make sure what is included and not. It is standard for florists to charge you hundreds of pounds for flowers and then not provide anything to put them in. It is a bit annoying. Another thing to check for is set up and break down fees. There may not be any but do make sure. There will undoubtedly be a delivery charge. Make sure this is not too steep and factor it into your budget. Make sure you get the price with VAT on top. You don't want an extra 20% on top of your bill. If you are hiring their vases then ask what happens if something is accidentally broken. The florist will want a deposit of ten to twenty-five per cent to secure your booking and then will want the full amount paid a couple of weeks before the wedding.

For some floral ideas check out myweddingflowerideas.co.uk

Be upfront about your budget. If you don't have a lot of money then be honest about this. The florist will know what flowers are cheaper and in season. A good florist will be able to work with whatever budget you have. They should be friendly and accommodating about it and if not immediately move on. The florist may not find your budget realistic. If they don't then think about it but don't be pressured. You don't need to hire a florist. Fortnum and Mason does beautiful flowers that are cheaper than most florists. You can even design your flowers yourself and buy them from a local florist without mentioning the 'W' word. Supermarkets also have beautiful flowers. I was very impressed by some flowers I saw in Sainsbury's and there was also some gorgeous flowers in Waitrose.

Orchids are also a great idea and can be bought very cheaply. I have seen some truly beautiful ones from £15. We had one at our wedding and it really added something special. You could also buy plants instead. They can work well if you get the right one. If another couple is getting married at the same venue as you then you could ask if they would like to share floral arrangements. As long as you can agree on colour and style you will be quids-in. Using a mirrored base can give the illusion of a larger arrangement. You do not have to go overboard with your flowers. A simple arrangement on each table will work and if it is a small wedding these do not have to be extravagant. You want guests to be able to see each other across the table.

If you get married around Valentine's Day, Mother's Day or Christmas then your flowers will probably cost a lot more money. This is not the florist's fault, flower wholesalers put the price up.

Once you decide on your florist give them the details of the venue manager or your wedding planner. They should sort everything else out for you in regards to delivery and setting up. You may have to source and deliver your own vases/containers however.

When buying your wedding flowers think about the venue's space and what guests will see. Brighten up any drab areas and highlight beautiful ones. If your venue is huge and spacious then vases with single roses will not pack much of a punch. You will need something more elaborate. A very good idea is to buy your flowers and then get your venue to turn them around. This won't work if you are using all of the rooms at every point but if the rooms are being turned around - this means your ceremony and reception is in one room and it gets 'turned around' by the venue in-between the two events while you and your guests go to another room - this can save money as you need to buy fewer flowers. Moving the flowers around really can get you value for money. If your ceremony and reception are in different places then it will also be possible to move your flowers to the next venue. Ask someone reliable to do this who you know will be careful and not break anything. Although accidents do happen and you want to factor in that possibility. You may want to inform your florist that you are going to do this however as they may need to arrange some flowers differently to work at both venues.

Flowers that are **good value all year** round include freesias, gerbera, roses, lisianthus and Singapore orchids.

What's in season …

Autumn: lilies, iris, phlox, roses, sweet pea, stock, berries, gerberas, hydrangea, calla lilies, fruits, alstroemeria, dahlia and sunflowers.

Winter: tulips, narcissi, lisianthus, roses, amaryllis, freesia, hydrangea, Singapore orchids and cymbidium orchids.

Spring: tulips, freesia, daffodils, hyacinths, lily of the valley, cherry blossom, anemone, agapanthus and hydrangea.

Summer: roses, phlox, peonies, iris, lilies, sweet pea, stock, agapanthus, hydrangea and delphiniums.

Adding something to suggest the season can also look stunning in a bouquet. You could either do this with colour or by adding berries or twigs for an autumn/winter wedding for instance.

If you are getting married in a church or another religious venue then make sure you know what the rules are. Churches can be very strict about decor.

Bouquet

The bouquet will probably be about £50. A shower bouquet, which cascades down, will cost even more £100-150. This is a lot of money for something that you throw away after a few hours but it does look great in pictures and there are ways to cut the cost.

Here are your options for the different bouquets: the previously mentioned **Shower** which cascades down and will cost a significant amount. It is wired to drop into a teardrop shape, **Posy**: this is the type of bouquet that my bridesmaids had. It is basically a smaller version of a hand tied bouquet. **Composites**: this is a flower which is made from lots of real petals which are wired together to make one big flower. **Crescent**: a flower and a flowering stem which are then wired together. Slender and classy. **Presentation**: an overarm bouquet. **Hand-tied**: a round bouquet composed of flowers, foliage and sometimes herbs. I had this for my bouquet and had some rosemary put it. Some brides get a specific bouquet for tossing. It doesn't have to match your original bouquet.

Posies for Bridesmaids

These should be like the bride's bouquet but smaller. About half or three-quarters of the size. They are usually the same flowers as the bride's bouquet and it looks great in pictures if they are.

Buttonhole

A buttonhole is a flower that goes through the buttonhole of the groom and other members of the wedding party's jacket. They are usually the groom, best man, ushers, bride's father and grooms father. The buttonhole is usually the same as one of the flowers in the bride's bouquet. So it looks like it was picked from there. Roses make great buttonholes. Buttonholes should be pinned on the left side and should be pinned on the underside of the lapel. No part of the actual pin should be showing. The flower should last the entire day and suit the outfit and personality of the groom.

Make sure the florist clearly states what buttonholes and corsages are for whom. Then make sure the venue know too and they can inform a member of the wedding party so they know where they are. Tell people they have one and then they can ask the venue themselves or an usher where to pick it up. You might want to order some extra buttonholes. Some might go missing or get damaged. If not, then you can give them out to some other men at the wedding. An alternative is getting the buttonholes and corsages delivered straight to the bride and groom. This will also stop any confusion.

Corsage

Sometimes the mother of the bride and the mother of the groom wear corsages, alongside some other members of the wedding party like flower girls. You can have a corsage that pins onto outfits, wristband corsages or floral headbands. If people don't want to ruin their expensive outfit then you can get corsages that stay in place thanks to a magnet.

For flower girls there is the traditional flower basket with petals that gets strewn from the basket. Make sure the petals don't get slippery and make someone fall down. Get the child to sprinkle gently, going from side to side of the aisle.

If you go for an alternative or an extra like a flowery headband then make sure this does not swamp the child. Take each child's age and size into consideration. You could get flowery headbands, a crown of flowers or a pomander which is a ball covered in flowers and lace. It hangs on the wrist from a strap. You could also put one flower in their hair or get a floral hair clip.

Centrepieces

Vases, beer glasses, glass milk bottles, jam jars…there are a few different options for your wedding flowers. You will, rather annoyingly, usually have to provide these yourself. I was lucky as I found beer glasses in Waitrose that were perfect. They came in a pack of four and only cost £4.50! I couldn't believe it. What a bargain and they looked like classy, beautiful vases. They are also not wasted now as we use them as glasses. Teacups, jars and jugs are also good choices that can look amazing. Depending on your venue and the theme of your wedding.

I did not get it right first time however. I bought some vases on Amazon, first checking with the florist, however it turns out they were not right after all as they wouldn't take the weight of the flowers and I couldn't send them back. Very annoying.

I have heard of people renting trees and large plants from nurseries. Apparently this is very cheap and can also cover anything at the venue that you really don't like. Many nurseries rent out a ficus or a palm amongst other trees and large plants. Do think hard about transportation though. It might be more trouble than it is worth. Another alternative is good old eBay, http://uk.ebid.net or a wonderful website where married couples sell their 'something old' called sellmywedding.co.uk You can pick up everything from centrepieces to accessories.

A tip if you are having plants or orchids is to buy a new container if the one you get them in looks drab or not very wedding-like. You can get beautiful silver pots from the pound store or in gardening shops for a very cheap price. A pound in the pound store, funnily enough.

If you have hay fever then try and buy some flowers that don't go for you. I find lilies make my hay fever much worse. Also think about guests and whether they have any allergies. Narcissi, hyacinths and freesias also tend to go for hay fever sufferers. Do people a favour if you know they are sufferers and either keep it away from them or choose different flowers.

The cost of wedding flowers is mostly due to the amount of labour involved. If your budget is low then ask the florist what type of arrangement and wedding flowers you could buy that are not too labour intensive. Alternatively, you can take a flower arranging course yourself or buy a book on the subject. This could save you a lot of money. Think of the time involved in your floral DIY project and the cost of the flowers before you go down this route. It might be fun and you could also give the wedding chore to a friend or family member who wants to help with the wedding. Most people love to get involved in weddings.

The truth is, you can pick flowers from your own garden or a friend's garden. You could also, with permission, pick them from a local nursery or buy them from a local flower market. Not mentioning the fact that they are for a wedding will stop people marking things up unnecessarily. Picking your own flowers and doing your own arrangement will not only be cheaper but will also have a wonderful personal touch. Many people hire a wedding florist because it is the done thing, but you really don't have to. Be brave and creative and you can have beautiful flowers at a much cheaper cost. Make sure you research the flowers you are working with and even ask a florist for help and advice. Some flowers will need to be stored in a certain way and some should not touch your skin so taking a class, buying a book or asking a friendly florist for some advice should prove invaluable.

If you want to keep your bouquet or buttonhole then there are a number of ways you can do so. For the buttonhole and smaller flowers you could get two pieces of tissue paper and put the buttonhole inside a heavy book and then place more heavy books on top. Leave for a few weeks and when you go back you will have a beautiful, pressed and dry flower that you can keep forever. You could also turn them into potpourri by taking the petals and then mixing them with oils and herbs. Put them in a jar for about six weeks and shake once a day.

You could also air-dry the bouquet and buttonhole by hanging them upside down in a dry, ventilated room. Separate the flowers for the best results. You could also preserve your wedding flowers with desiccants, you bury the flowers in silica gel which you can get from craft stores. This is easy to do.

You could also let your guests take some of the wedding flowers home so they don't go to waste. Or donate them to a church or a nursing home.

Throwing The Bouquet

Tradition goes that the person who catches the bouquet will be the next to get married. This usually means, even in modern times, that female guests take it quite seriously, or at least find it a bit of fun.

You obviously don't have to do this but some guests might be disappointed if you don't.

Alternatives

You don't need to have flowers, or even a floral bouquet. You can have one made of crystals or gems. I even saw one woman with toy cats as a bouquet and posies for the bridesmaids rather than flowers. It was an acquired taste but was certainly unique and also looked cute. You can get a bouquet made from buttons or brooches, feathers, candles, sea shells, sweets or origami. Bouquets made from fabric flowers can look beautiful and will also last forever. Silk flowers can also be used for centrepieces and bouquets. They can look beautiful and realistic. Candles are not expensive and can be bought very cheaply from IKEA or pound stores. You can float some tea lights in a bowl along with some flower heads. It can look very beautiful and adds ambience too. You could also have paper chains, origami and big- or small- letters that spell out love and the name of you and your spouse-to-be.

Another great idea is to have photos of the two of you and your life together dotted around the venue. You could also include pictures of all of the guests. It will spark conversation and make the guests get involved. Photographs from your childhood and pictures from the engagement party will have people entertained for a good amount of time. Especially if there is an entire life history memory board. A photo collage will work well but you could also hang them up on the wall with tiny clothes pegs. These are very cheap and the string won't cost much either. There are a good amount of wedding props on notonthehighstreet.com and you could also have a photo booth with lots of silly props to remind you of the day. You don't need to hire an expensive photo booth if you can't afford it, you could set a camera up and get guests to work it or buy lots of disposable cameras for guests to take pictures.

Bunting is very popular at weddings and can look great. It is also relatively inexpensive. If you are having an outdoor wedding or a summery wedding then this will look particularly good. There are specialist bunting stores but you can also get bunting from sellmywedding.com, eBay and Etsy. If you have some material and are good at sewing you could even make your own. You could also buy some material and then find a friend or an aunt with a sewing machine to make you some bunting. It is relatively easy for someone with sewing experience.

Another thing to think about is small baskets in the bathroom full of little essentials like hairspray, deodorant, spare tights, mints, soap, paracetamol and blister plasters. These are popular at weddings and always go down well. It can be a long day and these little things can make all of the difference to someone who needs one of the above.

Table Decoration

A good touch for the table decoration is a menu, a favour and a napkin on top of the serving plate. This looks very good and classy. Along with a floral centrepiece and some candles it is a simple but classic wedding look that always goes down a treat.

CHAPTER 13: MUSIC

Nothing sets the scene like music. It can create emotion, joy, happiness, sadness… the list is endless. Music isn't just for the dancing, the entire wedding will need music. I actually found this pretty intimidating at first. The crisis was averted however by my husband's Uncle Matthew offering to play during the ceremony and as the guests arrived. We then hired a DJ as I was worried about losing my iPod or it cutting out. I would also have had to buy certain music that I wanted and have someone watch the iPod and make sure the right song was played at the right time. This was all possibly but the DJ was 'only' £350 and this seemed reasonable to make sure everything went smoothly. Even more so as a family member was kind enough to pick up the bill.

DJ or Band?

That is the question. DJs are cheaper and take up less space but live music has its own ambience. The band may get funny about people requesting songs but the DJ won't. The band may want to be fed and watered as well. A bored DJ can ruin a party however, while a good one will create a great atmosphere. Let your preference, and your budget, decide.

Take your venue into consideration when deciding. While a DJ can fit into a small space, an orchestra will drown out a small venue and deafen your guests.

Choosing Your DJ

DJs can be very underrated. Okay a band is live music but a DJ can really create an atmosphere and get a party going. As for choosing a band, get recommendations. The venue will probably have their own or at least a preferred one. It may even be cheaper this way as many venues charge extra when you use outside suppliers. Our DJ was £350 in London. We thought this was quite reasonable. It is obviously still a lot of money but you may get a cheaper DJ if you do not live in London or are getting married off-peak. Make sure that the DJ has his own equipment or that the venue has some. This will avoid any extra hire charge fees on top. Many people are also DJs now. It is a popular thing to do so if you ask around you may have a friend, or a friend-of-a-friend who will do it for mates rates. Make sure you get along with the DJ and that he has good recommendations. Don't be scared to ask for feedback from former clients. The DJ will want a playlist, either an entire list of songs or just some suggestions and likes and dislikes. Also let him know what to play and when. You don't want to get the first dance song wrong.

Check to see if your DJ has played at your venue before, ask if they have any lights and how big their equipment is. Check whether or not you need to supply anything like a table.

We had a DJ at our wedding which went down a treat. I spent days putting together a playlist via Spotify. I then copy and pasted it into a word document. There are many wedding playlists on Spotify you can browse and then you can easily add the ones you like to a wedding playlist of your own. It is very easy to do and you can get a Spotify account for free if you don't mind the adverts. You can also do this on YouTube.

Being Your Own DJ

Most venues will have a sound system that will allow you to plug in an iPod or another device like a computer or an MP3 player. You can just load all of your favourite music onto your device or use Spotify which allows you access to lots of music either free with adverts or advert-free on a subscription basis. You could also use your iTunes and set it to automix so you get a transition between songs.

Put together a specific wedding playlist though so none of your cheesy guilty pleasures play during the wedding. You may never live it down. If you are using the venue's sound system then ask them how to work it. The sound is important and it will have to be decent. Make sure that you have good speakers, bought or hired if the venue does not have a sound system.

iPod

You can just make a playlist and plug your iPod in. This is a great way to save money. You will want to allocate a wedding party member who you trust to work the iPod and make sure it does not stop playing. You could ask people to do it in shifts and make sure that someone remembers to take it home at the end of the night and return it to you. If the mood changes you could get people to skip songs.

Spotify

Spotify is a music streaming service. It has a large library of music. They even have playlists which you can follow and there are a number of wedding ones there, as well as many ones on love and romance. Although the free version has adverts they give a free one-month trial so you know when to take it.

You will probably have to choose a lot of songs. You will need between fifty to eighty songs for four hours. That is a rough guide. On average a song lasts between three to five minutes.

Choosing Your Band

Live music is always great and will really get people up and dancing. Choose your band carefully. Ask for recommendations from friends.

Shortlisting Bands

The best thing to do is see them live, find out where they are playing and go see them. They should let you see them for free if you are thinking of booking them. If you cannot see them live then ask to see a video of them playing live. You don't want to be disappointed on the day.

Tracking Them Down

Word of mouth is one of the best ways but you can always check out bands on YouTube or go to some concerts. Popping 'wedding bands' into a search engine may also bring up the band of your dreams. Referrals are always good but make sure the band is to your taste.

As ever, recommendations are key. Ask around. After you have gotten some recommendations make sure you do a good amount of research. Search for the band, watch them perform on YouTube and check out their Facebook and Twitter profiles. They may also be on SoundCloud and that is a good way to hear some of their music. Make sure there are no negative comments about them anywhere. The internet makes the world a small place. If possible, go and see the band live. The band should be accommodating. It will also greatly help if you get along with the band. Make sure you won't have to deal with a jerk in the run up to your wedding and on the day. Make sure the band is approachable and that getting in touch with them is easy. Make sure you get everything in writing and have a contract. Don't pay a deposit until everything is agreed. Make sure you contact the band just before the wedding to go over everything with them. Make sure they have the phone number of a member of the wedding party in case they get lost or need to know anything. You don't want to be bothered on your wedding day.

After you have booked your band brainstorm with them. Ask them what they think will work and swap ideas. They may have some great song ideas but will also know if a song you have chosen is actually about a break up. Whitney Houston's *I Will Always Love You* (actually written by Dolly Parton) is a song most people want but it is actually a song about a break up. Pick some songs that you will want played but you can also let the band play whatever they think will suit the atmosphere. Giving them an idea of your tastes and ideas should be enough for them to get it right.

Providing a snack and some drinks for your band is a good idea but they should be coming in the evening so providing them with a meal is not usually done. Especially since they are not usually cheap and catering is expensive. It will also put them in a good mood and they will have more energy.

Find a band via wedding fairs, wedding magazines and blogs, the internet, pubs and clubs, suppliers and music agencies. Hiring music students is also an option. They will have less experience but will be cheaper and just as talented. Make sure they have insurance and good equipment. Also make sure they have some good recommendations.

Make sure the band does a sound check. A good one will insist but it is important to get the sound and volume right.

Most bands will want to be paid in full and will then charge after the wedding for any overtime. If you don't want to pay any overtime then make this clear with the band and have it in the contract. Otherwise you might leave and your friends might ask them to keep playing, leaving you with a big bill.

Wedding Playlist

Choosing your wedding playlist can be stressful, with lots of choice and little time. So to help get you started here is a starter wedding playlist. There are some really good songs here. Funnily enough, while researching wedding music I found out that 'Papa Was a Rolling Stone' by The Temptations is one of the most popular wedding songs. Hmm.

How Long Will I Love You – Ellie Goulding
All Of Me – John Legend
Can't Help Falling In Love With You – Elvis Presley -
When A Man Loves A Women – Percy Sledge
Ain't No Sunshine – Bill Withers
We Found Love – Rihanna & Calvin Harris
Chasing Cars – Snow Patrol
(I've Had) The Time Of My Life – Bill Medley & Jennifer Warnes
Ed Sheeran – Kiss Me
Adele – Make You Feel My Love
Marry You – Bruno Mars
Just Like A Star – Corinne Bailey Rae
You've Got The Love – Florence & The Machine
Rule The World – Take That
Everything I Do (I Do It For You) – Bryan Adams
You Do Something To Me – Paul Weller
God Only Knows – The Beach Boys
Just Say Yes – Snow Patrol
Don't Want To Miss A Thing – Aerosmith
Your Song – Elton John
At Last – Etta James
Come What May – Ewan McGregor & Nicole Kidman
The Way You Look Tonight – Frank Sinatra
Let's Get It On – Marvin Gaye
So Here We Are – Bloc Party
Iris – The Goo Goo Dolls
We Have All The Time In The World – Frank Sinatra
Better Together – Jack Johnson
Happy – Pharrell
Endless Love – Lionel Richie & Diana Ross
You And Me – Lifehouse
Sex On Fire – Kings Of Leon
Truly, Madly, Deeply – Savage Garden
Heaven – DJ Sammy & Yanou
When I Fall In Love – Nat King Cole

Isn't She Lovely – Stevie Wonder
I'm Not In Love – 10cc
Your Song – Elton John
Midnight Train To Georgia – Gladys Knight and The Pips
What a Difference A Day Makes – Dinah Washington
My Baby Just Cares For Me – Nina Simone
I'll Stand By You – Pretenders
I Will Always Love You – Whitney Houston (Do keep in mind that this is actually a break up song)
Moon River – Audrey Hepburn
Take My Breath Away – Berlin
You're Still The One – Shania Twain
I Don't Want To Miss a Thing – Aerosmith
Just The Way You Are- Bruno Mars
Marry Me - Train
Diamonds - Rihanna
Save The Best For Last - Vanessa Williams
Come To Me - Goo Goo Dolls
My First, My Last, My Everything - Barry White
Baby, it's you - The Beatles
When Loves Takes Over - David Guetta Featuring Kelly Rowland
Adore You - Miley Cyrus
Home - Edward Sharpe And The Magnetic Zeros

Just as important as the playlist is the Don't Play list. Songs that are associated with an ex or a bad memory should be avoided at all costs, even if requested by a guest. Make sure you both put a list together and give it to the band/DJ.

Special Requests

Your guests will probably make some special requests. Most people will have no problem with this and we certainly didn't. It can add to the evening and make people feel included. If one of the songs is on the 'don't play' list, just get your DJ/band to politely say this.

First Dance

Your first dance song should have meaning to you. It should be your song or one that has meant a lot during your relationship. Pick it carefully as it will be then forever associated with your love for each other and your marriage. Choose something classic that you don't think you will get sick of. It would also help if you choose something that you can actually dance too. You don't have to choose one song. You can start off with a slow ballad and then break out into a jazz routine. YouTube is full of videos of couples doing impressive first wedding dances, sometimes with the wedding party joining in. One where the bride and groom recreated the famous scene from Dirty Dancing went viral a couple of years ago and they ended up in all of the papers and a number of magazines too.

Don't worry too much about making a fool of yourself. Even if you just do a slow shuffle and then get the maid of honour and the best man to join in. If you are really nervous then take some lessons or hire a dance teacher. Just practicing around the house with your spouse-to-be in a pair of shoes similar to the ones you will wear on the day will help. Take into account your dress too. You might not be able to move very much in it.

Choosing Your Song

Many couples already have a song but if you don't it can be a little daunting. In fact, you may want to choose something different anyway if your original song is not easy to dance to, or just too personal. Listen to lots of songs and choose something you both like which has no negative connotations.

Dancing

You might want to take a couple of lessons If you have two left feet or even just having some anxiety. My husband and I kept meaning to practice and watch some YouTube videos but we never found the time.

Dancing With Parents

There is a huge trend right now for extravagant first dances that are then uploaded to YouTube. Another trend is brides dancing with their fathers and less common is grooms dancing with their mothers.

These can be fun but take into consideration your dancing skills, a lack of time to rehearse and nerves on the day. However, if you want to set yourself a challenge, then go for it. Just make sure it does not upstage the bride or groom, they are who the entire day is supposed to be about.

OTHER ENTERTAINMENT

Performers

You could hire some dancers or if it is a themed wedding, some performers to set the tone, flapper girls for a 1920s wedding for instance.

Ceilidh

Scottish dancing is always fun. Even people who are generally not good dancers can manage a fling.

Games

Some super-sized games could be fun and break down social barriers.

Photo Booth

Photo booths have become very popular in recent years. As are keeping some props in the booth so guests can let their hair down and get a bit silly. You could also set one up yourself if you cannot afford a proper one. Just ask a trusted friend to work your camera or bring their own and do it for an hour as a wedding present. You could also set up a little area with props and a backdrop and have disposable cameras everywhere. This might cost you a lot of money to develop the film but could leave you with a lot of wonderful memories.

Magician

Unlike the magicians of old, today's magicians like Dynamo really add a whole new dimension and level of fun to magic. Far from being cheesy, the right magician can make your wedding fun and memorable but the wrong one will just feel flat and cheesy. Get one from www.themagiccircle.co.uk

Artist

A caricaturist always goes down a treat. It also leaves guests with a rather amazing keepsake. A friend of mine, Rich Nairn, is the most talented caricaturist that I know and has drawn everyone from Ricky Gervais to Martin Scorsese. Oh, and me. If you hire him you won't regret it and I am not being biased. I interviewed him and his biography and answers are below.

Rich Nairn was born in 1975 and has been doodling away as long as he can remember. What used to get him in trouble with his teachers is now his full time profession. Rich has been drawing cartoons, illustrations and caricatures for a living now for 15 years and hasn't looked back. You will find Rich at events throughout the UK drawing caricatures, and can follow him on twitter: @richnairn, where you will find him posting all sorts of random doodles and artwork.

Tell us about what you do.

I travel across England drawing caricatures at events and most of these are weddings.

Basically, I attend a wedding for up to four hours, drawing the guests. This provides the same sort of entertainment and laughs you would get from a magician with the added bonus that the guests have a memento to take away with them.

How many weddings have you done?

I work roughly 60 weddings a year and have been doing this for about 17 years. In 2007 I realised this was taking over my life so started full time. An exact number would be over 1000, that's all I know.

What is the best thing about being a caricaturist?

It's great when you get people that really enjoy a caricature. At most weddings I attend there will be one group of people that I remember as they laugh so hard. A reaction like this only serves to boost my confidence and therefore makes the pictures funnier.

How do guests react? I imagine most people want their portrait done.

With nearly all it's different degrees of laughter, with the occasional shock. Some are scared, maybe from a previous bad experience with a caricaturist and it's nice to change their opinion. Caricatures are supposed to be fun, not offensive.

What are your packages?

For most weddings I work a 4 hour time slot, and price packages differ depending on the county. A google map on the bookings page of my site gives a price for these packages.

What questions should couples ask you before the big day?

They should make sure times have been confirmed with me, and discuss with me the best time slot for me to work. I can work most parts of the day and depending on the venue, amount of guests and generally how their day flows a different time slot can make all the difference.

How many drawings can you do at a wedding?

In a four hour slot I draw between 30 to 50 caricatures. Obviously the amount depends on the amount of people in each drawing.

What kind of things do the bride and groom ask for?

The bride and groom will ask some of the questions listed above, with the addition of "can I keep hold of the pictures and hand them to the bride and groom at the end?" This isn't something I often do, as I find handing the caricatures out creates a buzz as people pass them around. One option is for me to take photos of people with their caricatures which I then add to a gallery on my Facebook page. The bride, groom and guests can then take a look at everyone's pics in the days following the wedding.

What is your favourite wedding you have ever done?

That's a tough question, there's been so many different themes and crowds over the years. Every one has something unique. For myself, if the crowd is great and they love what I do then that becomes my favourite wedding ever, for that night. Then a week or two later I'm thinking the same once more.

Describe an average day at a wedding for us.

An average day varies on what time slot I'm there for. Generally, my process is to arrive at the wedding a few minutes before I start to get my bearings. Then I introduce myself to the bride and groom and begin drawing them as they wander among their guests. After that it's picking good faces to draw. Once a few pictures are circulating it then becomes a race to get round and draw as many as I can get through in my time.

What is your favourite thing about doing weddings?

It's just the most wonderful way to earn a living. To be a part of the biggest day of someone's life is such an honour and to watch the smiles on people's faces as I reveal their doodles. I couldn't think of anything I would rather do.

Thanks, Rich

Fireworks

Can be an expensive option but will certainly start (or finish) the night off with a bang. Literally. The fireworks you can have will obviously depend on where the wedding is held.

Lookalikes

Hiring a lookalike for the party part of your wedding can add some fun. It can be quite unusual to have Brad Pitt walking around your reception! The guests will certainly have something to talk about and have their picture taken with. This may be too 'party' or glitzy for some people but go ahead if it is what you want. It would certainly be fun.

Karaoke

Your venue might not have a licence for karaoke so check first. You can hire a karaoke set if your venue doesn't have one or you are getting married in a 'dry' space like a marquee. This will certainly make your wedding fun and memorable, if not a little embarrassing for some.

A Slideshow

If you have the technology for this it can be a wonderful touch.

CHAPTER 14: ALCOHOL

Your venue may not allow you to bring in your own alcohol but if they do then this is an area where you can save. Some venues let you bring in your own wine but will charge a corkage fee. It is good to do this as long as the corkage fee is not too high.

Corkage

The corkage fee is the amount of money the venue charge to remove the cork from your wine and serve it. You must watch out for corkage. Some corkage fees are expensive, as much as £12 per bottle. Take this into consideration because it really does add up. We spent more money on corkage than actual alcohol at our wedding.

We got our wine imported from a wonderful organic farm in Tuscany called Fattoria La Villa. A number of guests said it was the best wine they had ever had at a wedding. Not surprising considering how many awards Fattoria have won for their wine. We did a general review of their amazing food and wine here: http://www.frost-magazine.com/2013/09/fattoria-la-vialla-review-organic-italian-food-fresh-from-the-farm/

We got prosecco instead of champagne. Far from being a cheap version of champagne it can taste better, is a lot cheaper and is easier on the head as it has fewer bubbles. A great alternative for those on a budget. If you have a big budget and still want champagne then I recommend Sainsbury's Blanc de Blancs Brut NV Champagne which is amazing and costs £22.50 per bottle (although it tends to be cheaper around about Christmas time when Sainsbury's drop the price) or if you really want to blow your budget: Taittinger champagne. The Taittinger Prélude Grands Crus NV is especially divine but cost upwards from £49 per bottle.

The best time to stock up on champagne/prosecco/cava is at Christmas time. This is when supermarkets cut their price. Buy in bulk and you will save a fortune.

Another tip to save money is to have cocktails at your wedding. We had Buck's Fizz (prosecco and orange juice) and Bellini's (peach puree and prosecco) but you can mix sparkling wine with most things or even make a special cocktail for your big day and name it something sweet and personal. This is a nice touch that guests will remember. You will probably also want to keep the recipe handy to share it with guests.

Other Tips to Keep Your Alcohol Bill Down

Keep the reception short.
Buying in bulk always make things cheaper.
Cut the number of guests.

Go to France and buy in bulk. A surprisingly cheap option and you don't have to pay any tax as long as it is for personal use or a gift.
Wine clubs and retailers such as Naked Wine or Virgin Wine tend to have good deals.
Don't be scared to go into your off-licence and ask for advice. If you are buying in bulk they could also cut you a good deal. If not then just go somewhere else.

The venue might not let you bring in your own alcohol, if not then make sure it is worth going with that venue. Some venues are reasonable but others will over-charge. Ask them what is inclusive of the venue charge or what you will be charged extra for. You don't want any nasty surprises after the wedding.

Cash Bars

Although very few people can afford to pay for large quantities of alcohol for hundreds of people all day, you should make sure your guests get some free drinks. However, a cash bar in the evening or if they want something off-menu is fine.

ALCOHOL LOGISTICS: So, how much do you need?

How Much Alcohol To Buy

At our wedding we had more bottles of wine than guests, and some of those guest were teetotal, not old enough to drink or driving home so were taking it easy. Despite this the amount of alcohol we had left at the end of the night was zero. A bit of a bitch on the corkage fee but we were just glad our guests had a good time. So here is my advice: never underestimate how much people drink because it is A LOT.

During the wedding breakfast, guests will generally drink half a bottle of wine each. Have a mix of red and white on the table. We also included rosé which was a huge hit. However some guests won't drink, or will drink more or less. Drivers, for example, will be drinking less. Obviously if you have invited children to your wedding they will need soft drinks.

A standard bottle of champagne of 75ml gives six champagne flute glasses.
A bottle of wine generally gives five glasses of wine.
A litre of alcohol will break down into 40 shots.

If you are really struggling then there are alcohol calculators online. All you have to do is put in the amount of guests and then what they like to drink, it then does the hard work. Put 'alcohol calculator' into a search engine.

Bar

You can have an open bar or a paying bar, or even combine the two. Although some people complain about having to pay for a drink at a wedding, caring, decent people will know that you are not rich and should understand if they have to pay for a few drinks.

At our wedding we bought a lot of wine but if guests wanted anything else other than that they had to pay. We thought this was fair as we didn't have a lot of money and had already supplied tea, coffee, soft drinks, a three course meal and a considerable amount of wine.

Prosecco

Prosecco is very underrated. It is cheaper than champagne and has fewer bubbles so you don't get as drunk. Prosecco is a sparkling wine from Italy, much like champagne is a sparkling wine from the champagne region in France and cava is a sparkling wine from Spain. It is possible to get a wonderful prosecco that is reasonably priced and your friends will not think that you went for the cheaper choice. Just choose carefully. We got our prosecco straight from Italy and made sure we tried a bottle first. It went down a treat and our guests loved it.

CHAPTER 15: THE CAKE

The craziness of the wedding industry really shows up in the price of wedding cakes. When my fiancé and I first started looking, we couldn't find one for less than £350, and most of them weren't even nice. If you take away the fact they have the word 'wedding' in front of them, would anyone actually pay thousands of pounds for a cake? I think not. In saying that, there are a lot out there with the craftsmanship and design that makes the price worthwhile. If you want great design at a good price then I recommend going the supermarket route. My fiancé and I got our wedding cake from Waitrose. Marks And Spencer also do great, affordable wedding cakes.

When buying a wedding cake make sure you check how many people it serves. The website should tell you or ask your baker. Another thing to check is if decoration is included. Some cakes look amazing but the small print says that the decoration is not included. This is also an easier way to get a cheaper cake, if you decorate it yourself, it costs less. Although there is the added stress.

While researching wedding cakes I saw a lot of gorgeous wedding cake toppers on eBay and ribbon is very cheap to buy from a haberdashery. You could also make your own or get a relative to make one. Although I would not do this if you are not brilliant at baking. Waitrose.com also have some guides on decorating your wedding cake and the BBC also have a great blog on making your own wedding cake on their website.

You can let your imagination really go with the cake. You don't need to have the traditional fruit mix or sponge. You could have a cheesecake or a chocolate cake. There is an amazing selection of wedding cakes. Unfortunately most of them cost an astronomical amount of money. A 'cheap' wedding cake will be at least £230. Depressing.

One way of getting a cheaper wedding cake without compromising on what you want would be to design your own and then take it to a local baker and try to do a deal with them. Don't just go with the first baker, ask around and get different quotes. Also make sure their customers are happy with them. They need to be able to deliver the cake on time. You will usually have to pick up the wedding cake before the wedding day but you could ask about delivery. You will probably need to get a trusted relative or one of the wedding party to pick up the cake and deliver it to the venue.

You may also have a relative who is an excellent baker or has a skill at cake decoration. Most people love weddings and are happy to get involved so offer to pay for the ingredients and then ask them to make you the cake as a wedding gift.

Hopefully they will be flattered. Make sure they are up to the task and can work to a deadline.

Another option is to buy plain white cakes from a supermarket or a baker and then stack them up. You could then decorate these yourself and add a cake topper. Adding fresh flowers like some roses is also a good touch that really looks beautiful.

Keep a look out for deals as well. Many supermarkets run deals on cakes, especially in summer.

Another good idea is to get a mixed filling. This gives guests a choice as not everyone will like a fruit mix. We went for a mix of vanilla sponge and fruit. It was a traditional choice but it went down a treat.

Many couples also stack cupcakes on a stand rather than having a cake. This can look great and would also be easy for relatives to do. You could ask a few people to make cupcakes for you or even make your own. Try and follow the same recipe and have a clear vision on what you want the finished product to look like. It helps if everyone uses the same icing.

You can also have a cheese tower. This is basically a tower of cheese which is done well and has decoration. It can be served as a cheese course during your wedding and is perfect for those who are more savoury than sweet. It is also good for diabetics. Waitrose and Marks and Spencer do one and you can also put 'wedding cheese towers' or another variation into a search engine.

Another option is to have a tower of macaroons. They are delicious and it will look very chic. This could be a cone shaped tower and the macaroons would be attached to it.

For your cake topper you could also get a personalised cake topper made of you and your other half. Quite a number of companies now make these and prices generally start at £100 for one made of sugar. If you want one that is more permanent and that costs less, non-edible ones start at about £45.

To save costs you can also serve the wedding cake as dessert. Most guests won't be able to handle both anyway and a lot of the wedding cake tends to not get eaten. Which can feel quite sad, especially when it costs so much.

Of course, you don't need to have a wedding cake. You could make a dessert station instead, full of all of your favourite sweets. It is your wedding, you can do whatever you want.

Another way to save costs is to have a 'dummy layer'. Many cake designers will do this and it is a good idea if you are in a big venue but your budget is tight. A dummy layer or tier is made of polystyrene but looks edible and is decorated. Tell your caterer about it before they cut it up so the poor things don't get confused when they are trying to cut through it.

Finding a Cake Designer

Finding the perfect cake designer might sound daunting at first but there are plenty of resources out there to help you find the perfect person to make your dream wedding cake. Have a browse on online wedding directories that have a good reputation and in wedding magazines such as Brides. Pinterest will certainly have pictures of beautiful wedding cakes which will hopefully have a credit, and if you are very lucky, a link to the cake maker, wedding blogs will also have some recommendations. Another tip is to go to a wedding exhibition such as Brides: The Show.

Your local baker may also make amazing wedding cakes and will (hopefully) be cheaper than a top-of-the-range wedding cake designer and may also be just as good.

Top tip: You don't have to purchase your wedding cake from your caterer. You can ask them to cut the cake you do buy though. They may charge a fee for this. Our amazing caterer, The Pickled Fork, didn't, but make sure you find out in advance if there will be an extra fee and how much it will be.

As with most things to do with weddings it is best to have an idea of what you want, which means collecting clippings from magazine and photos on your iPad. Have pictures of your venue, your flowers and other things that you think will be relevant. Keep your colour scheme in mind. Our wedding cake was pale pink, white and pale green which matched our wedding colours, apart from the blue in our flowers and bridesmaids' dresses.

Another tip when wedding cake shopping is to eat cake! Yes, don't just sample the wedding cake of designers you test out (although that is fun) but also try out different cake flavours when you eat out or if you see any in shops or bakeries. You might come across a wonderful flavour or unique twist that you would never have thought of otherwise.

It is also worth trying to book your cake designer early, as many of the really good ones will get booked up early, especially if you are getting married in peak season.

You don't have to book a cake designer who lives near you, many will do taste tests by mail. This will be more stressful though, so think hard if you could handle the stress of your wedding cake, or the samples going missing.

When using a search engine good terms to use are 'wedding cake designer', 'wedding cake designer pro', 'custom wedding cakes design' 'good wedding cake designers', 'wedding cakes designer online' or 'bespoke wedding cake".

Many high-end cake designers will not allow anything on a cake that is not edible so keep this in mind. If you would like flowers on your cake you can still have them, just choose ones that are edible or have your designer make flowers from icing.

Ask the designer if they will assemble it when it is delivered or if you will have to get someone else to do this. This is usually the caterer or your wedding planner. Also ask what they will deliver the cake on, some provide a silver tray, others just a piece of cardboard.

Your wedding planner or venue manager should liaise with the cake designer to arrange delivery and set up, which should be a good few hours before the wedding. Make sure the cake is up to the task.

Cake Stand

This is another thing you have to think about. We were lucky as our venue came with a beautiful cake stand and a knife. It is these little things that you have to keep in mind when planning a wedding.

If your venue does not have a cake stand you can use you can hire one from a local baker or buy one second hand.

SUPERMARKETS

Waitrose

Waitrose do an amazing range of wedding cakes that are reasonably priced. Well, reasonable when you consider how much other cakes cost. They also have the Royal cake maker Fiona Cairns making a wedding range for them. We got our wedding cake from Waitrose and it not only looked stunning but it tasted delicious. We didn't even need a topper as there was a beautiful rose detail that started at the top of the cake and worked its way down.

Other supermarkets like Marks & Spencer also make their own wedding cakes. They have a very good selection and even have one you can build yourself tier by tier. The tiers range from £8-30 with an extra-large tier priced at £44. We have not tasted any of Marks & Spencer's cakes but I reckon they would be just as nice.

Making Your Own

If you are a good baker then you could make your own wedding cake. There are a lot of great videos on YouTube that could help. Just keep in mind that this will take up a lot of time and won't necessarily be cheaper due to the fact that you will have to do a test run and might have to make the cake a few times.

This will be a great talking point at the wedding and the sense of accomplishment will be an amazing feeling.

Flowers are a great idea when it comes to decoration and are relatively inexpensive. Just make sure they are free from pesticides and are removed before the cake is cut up. Roses in particular look beautiful.

Size And Serving

If you buy a cake from a supermarket it should say online how many people it serves. If not, ask. This is important information. If you are having a small wedding you will need a smaller cake, which will cost less.

Tell your baker or cake maker how many guests there will be. Also remember that not everyone will eat cake.

As a general guide a two tier cake will give roughly 60 portions. A three tier cake will give roughly 70 portions, a four tier cake will give about 130 portions. This is based on average sizing and may differ from cake to cake. Ask your baker or cake designer.

We had our wedding cake displayed in the reception on a beautiful cake stand. It really added to the venue and the guests liked it.

Cutting The Cake

While the picture of the bride and groom cutting the cake may be a wedding cliché, many guests still look forward to witnessing this ritual. One of my favourite pictures of my wedding is one that my bridesmaid Holly took of my husband James and I cutting the cake. Just because something is a cliché doesn't mean it shouldn't be done.

The cake used to be a symbol of the couple's first meal together. It was a sign that the wedding was over as the bride and groom would then leave.

You can cut the cake before dinner so it is served as dessert (we did this) or you can cut it just before everybody hits the dance floor. Just make sure it is announced as many guests will want to take pictures. There is also a superstition that the bride should cut the first piece or remain childless, considering I found out I was pregnant two weeks after my wedding this certainly would not have applied to me! It is up to you if you want to follow this tradition or not.

If you are into tradition then the right way to cut the cake is that the groom places his hand over the bride's as she holds the knife, they then cut a small piece from the back of the bottom tier of the cake. The groom then feeds the bride a piece of cake and then vice versa.

After you have cut the cake the venue will take it into the kitchen to be cut up for the guests and then served.

Saving The Top Tier

It is traditional to keep the top tier of the cake and freeze it for the christening of the first child. Obviously this does not have to be done. Many people are not religious or traditional and others don't want to have children. Another reason couples save the top tier is to eat it on their first wedding anniversary. This is another cute idea.

If you do save the top tier make sure you freeze it properly. You don't want any mould or freezer burns. Make sure the venue/caterer knows that you want to keep the top tier or they might cut it up with the rest of the cake. If you are going straight off on your honeymoon then ask a trusted friend to take it home and freeze it for you until you come back from your honeymoon.

Your cake designer will be able to tell you how to safely freeze your wedding cake. If you buy it from a supermarket it should also have clear instructions. Ring their customer service department if you are unsure of anything.

CHAPTER 16: CATERING

It cannot be overestimated how important catering is. That doesn't mean you need to spend a fortune. Catering is usually one of the main wedding expenses but there are ways to keep costs down. If guests are going to be with you all day then you must feed them and make sure the food is good.

When I was trying to find a caterer the fact that I live in London, and had my wedding there, really worked against me. Many caterers had on their website that they did not want to be contacted if your budget was under two thousand pounds or under a certain amount of people. Stress. But everything is achievable so I started being more creative. Friends helped and also made some great suggestions. One was that Marks And Spencer make great party food. As do Waitrose and many other supermarkets. It would be very easy to feed your guests with great food without spending too much if you did it this way. A great tip for saving money is to do two courses and then have the wedding cake as the third course.

My main idea, and the one I did want to go with, was to do a wedding hamper. Each table would have a wedding hamper for a certain amount of guests, in the hamper would be lots of wonderful things like Parma ham, cheese, bread, wine, sandwiches, salami and various other fresh foods and drinks. We thought it would be fun and get everyone involved but we made the mistake of asking for opinions from a few family members who were negative about it and ended up not doing it. I still think it would have been amazing though. Each guest would also have gotten some stuff to take away and we would have gotten the best food and imported some stuff from this organic farm we love in Tuscany called Fattoria La Villa. This is where we got our wedding wine and many of the guests said it was the best wine they had ever had at a wedding.

We also found a company that will send individual hampers to a venue. Many companies also do picnic food which they will deliver to a specific place. Depending on your wedding and the theme you can save money by thinking outside of the box and also give your guests an experience they will never forget.

For ideas check out food blogs, think about your favourite food, favourite restaurants and go through cookbooks. When choosing take in the season of your wedding. Hot soup on a hot summer's day may not fit but at a winter wedding would be greatly appreciated. Have lighter food for a summer wedding. Most weddings have fish, chicken, lamb or beef along with a vegetarian option. Don't see this as a bad thing as these are what people usually like to eat. Think mass catering. That doesn't mean you have to compromise on quality or fun. If you can't decide on what dessert you want then you could have a dessert table.

All of this leads me to my amazing caterer: The Pickled Fork. We found the Pickled Fork because my sister-in-law, Alexandra, used to work for a pop up restaurant and met the guys who run it. She contacted them initially and then we met Alex in a pub and struck a deal. So with catering it helps to contact smaller, up and coming chefs and companies that are doing pop ups and catering. You will be surprised at the amazing food you can get for a fraction of what you would have to pay a bigger company.

Other great ideas include taking your guests to your favourite restaurant (depending on whether they can do the numbers and will give you a good deal), an afternoon tea party, a barbecue, a finger buffet, a burger or pie van, fish and chips, hog roast, pancakes, tapas, sushi or even street food. You could even do the catering yourself with the help of friends and family if you think you are talented enough and have nerves of steel. My husband wanted to do this initially and I panicked until I managed to talk him out of it. If you decide on doing your own catering then keep the recipe simple and make sure you have a lot of helpers on hand. Make sure you have somewhere to store the food and to transport it. Make sure it is cooked and heated properly. Food poisoning is not what you or your guests want on your wedding day. Hire some waiters too. You could even get them cheaply if you hire some students or maybe pay some cousins.

You could also try a culinary school. Some of their former students might be able to do a wedding cheaply, they may have an association or something. Post a 'caterer wanted' on their bulletin board.

This all depends on your venue however. Some venues will not allow you to bring food or drink in and some will charge more for an outside caterer. Although, if you are just bringing food in and not an actual caterer this is something worth negotiating over. Make sure you find out what is allowed before you book the venue. Venues who offer in-house catering packages can be a lot cheaper, especially if you book them off-season.

Get recommendations before you book your caterer. Make sure you search online for any information too. Bad reputations spread and in this day and age of social media and the internet it becomes easy to sort the good from the bad. You could also contact previous customers through social media. Make sure you meet your caterer in person and go with your gut, do you like them and trust them? Do they look clean and tidy?

What To Ask The Caterer

Has your caterer worked at your venue before?
What kind of experience do they have?
Do they do big or small weddings?
How many weddings have they done?
Can they work well in the space provided?
Do they only do weddings with a certain number of guests? Some caterers will specify a minimum amount of guests.
Ask for a tasting, ask to see sample menus and photographs of previous weddings if possible.

Ask for previous clients' information so you can ask them some questions. Ask them if expensive items were sparse, if the food looked and tasted good, were staff prompt and professional? Did the caterer do a good job? What, if any, negative comments they have.
What kind of food do they specialise in? If they are not known for the type of food you want then it might be better to go somewhere else.

Talk through exactly what you want. Whether it be a sit down meal, canapés, three-courses or just two with the wedding cake served at the end. Decide if you want it to be formal or more casual. Will you want tea and coffee served afterwards? If you are on a budget then let your caterer know. They should be able to work with your budget in mind and will certainly be able to cut some costs by choosing cheaper options like seasonal food and less expensive cuts of meat. If they are rude about it then immediately go with another caterer. You want someone who is on your side.

Ask for details on pricing. Then you can see what can be cut and what is costing a lot of money. Ask as many questions as possible and get a full quotation in writing. Check if VAT is included.

If you are getting married in a marquee or a barn then the caterer may have to bring their own cooking facilities. This will probably cost more so do check.

Decide if the venue or the caterer is supplying the alcohol, or if you are supplying your own. Make sure you get the best deal. Will the venue charge to serve the alcohol? Corkage fees can really add up.

Can you bring in your own wedding cake and will the venue charge to serve it?

Check whether the price includes staff and if they provide crockery, cutlery, napkins, tables and chairs if your venue does not. Also ask about breakage charges. Reasonable breakage should be included in the price. A ratio of one waiter per ten people works.

What is the hourly rate of the staff and is a tip included?

Will the caterer provide menus? How much will they charge for this?

Ask if they are working on any other jobs on the day of your wedding. Might not matter but good to know.

Will the catering staff help set up the room? Will they charge more? How long will it take?

Can they cater to every dietary requirement: vegan, vegetarian, allergies or food for kids?

Will they supply food for other wedding suppliers? Would they do it for a reduced rate and how much notice will they need?

Tasting

A smaller, pop-up chef might not be able to do a tasting but you should be able to go along to one of their events prior to your wedding. Just like you try on your wedding dress before you buy it, I don't think it is reasonable for a caterer to not at least give a little bit of a taster. You need to know what the food tastes like. Catering is not cheap either so be firm with them. Most should offer one anyway. If this is not okay then maybe if they are doing an event they could prepare a take-away box for you to try. Don't bring too many people to the tasting. It will probably just be you and your fiancé but having too many opinions might not help nor be fair to the caterer. If the tasting is bad then beware. If the caterer cannot cook a good meal for you and your fiancé, then the chance of them cooking a good meal for a hundred guests is pretty low. Make sure the food will be served in the same way on your wedding day. Presentation is important.

When tasting try and taste with the wine you will have on the day. Either bringing your own or ordering some through the caterer. Write down suggestions and ask for any changes that you want. Make sure you write it all down. Your caterer might be working on more than one project at the time.

Buffets

Usually, but not always, a cheaper option. It may also be a couple of hundreds of pounds cheaper but significantly less quality. If you are on a budget the entire thing will also probably be cold but not always. Despite the criticism a buffet can really work and is also less old-fashioned than a sit-down three-course meal. Guests will mingle more and there will be a good variety. You could also make your own buffet so it really could cut your costs. Another great thing about a buffet is that you can cut down on waiting staff. Guest get their own food so it works out cheaper but you will still need staff. Don't underestimate or overestimate how much your guests will eat. You don't want too many leftovers or anyone going hungry.

You can have staff behind a long table serving out the food or just have the food out so guests can help themselves. You will need some staff either way. To make sure there are no long queues you can ask certain tables to go first or have more than one food station dotted around. Make sure you make/buy some menus to let people know what the options are.

Cocktails

Cocktails are always a huge hit and you could make up your own to celebrate your wedding day. Cocktails are also a brilliant way to make your alcohol go further and cut costs. Bellini's and Buck's Fizz will cut down your champagne bill.

The Wedding Breakfast is so called because it is the first meal of your married life together.

Nibbles

Think about your guests and their blood-sugar levels. If there is a long stretch between the ceremony and lunch then make sure you have some biscuits or nibbles handy. They don't have to be expensive but you don't want your guests fainting.

Canapés

Great if you can afford them. Keep in mind that guests will be having a full meal later so keep canapés light and make sure they can be eaten with one bite and easily so. Try and mix it up, so if you are having fish for your main, choose something different for your canapés. Canapés are usually included in the package or priced per person or canapé. Make sure they are cost-effective and include vegetarian options. For a ninety minute reception have between six and eight canapés per person.

Tea and Coffee

Tea and coffee is a great idea at a wedding. If your wedding lasts all day it is better to not have everyone drunk. Tea and coffee is a digestive too and great after a meal.

Considering Dietary Requirements

Many people these days have some kind of dietary requirement. Whether it is gluten, wheat, dairy or meat, pleasing everyone may be hard. It helps to know what you are dealing with prior to deciding on your menu so ask your guests if they have any special dietary requests. Put the vegetarian option on the menu and make sure you make a note for the caterer and let the waiting staff know where they will be sitting.

Vegetarians

Make sure you find out if any of your friends have any specific dietary requirements. It helps to include this on the invitation so people can email you. Many people are now vegetarian or vegan and there are also a lot of people who cannot eat gluten or dairy. Let your caterer know in advance and include this information in the seating plan or make a separate list for your caterer and the venue. This will also make it easier for the waiters.

Our wedding caterer was **The Pickled Fork**. **Alex Motture** is an amazing chef and many of our guests said it was the best wedding food they had ever had in their life.

The presentation of his food was also amazing. I have an interview with him below. Check out his site at http://www.thepickledfork.com

How did you get into wedding catering?

I first got into wedding catering whilst working at Mustard Catering 4 years ago. Although I had catered for weddings in the past it was not on the same scale.

Tell us about the Pickled Fork

Here at The Pickled Fork we are all about using the best of British seasonal produce whether it be from the land, sea or sky. We host weekly pop up restaurants around London and are also involved with local breweries and distilleries.

What is the most important thing to get right?

For me the most important thing to get right is your timing. If you don't get this right things can spiral out of control very quickly

What should couples look for in a wedding caterer?

Couples looking for a wedding caterer should be keeping an eye out for someone with flair, patience, attention to detail, a passion for food and a strong background in hospitality.

What kind of questions should a couple ask their caterer?

A couple of questions that I think should be asked would be: How much, and are you flexible on price!?

Talk us through a day catering for a wedding.

Slightly tricky question as every wedding is different therefore no two days in the kitchen will be the same. Although generally the day will generally run the same depending on what style of menu the couple have chosen. It will usually involve an early start and a late finish with lots of prep in between.

What kind of food do you recommend for weddings?

It all depends on what the couple want. Probably the most straightforward and least problematic from my point of view would be a hot and cold buffet. Another good option is to have sharing platters placed on the table and the guests help themselves.

What about seasonal weddings? What food is better for summer rather than winter?

Definitely menus should be based on seasons. There is no point putting a braised ox cheek with root vegetable dish on in the middle of summer. Food should match the time of year, that way it keeps it simple and the ingredients can shine.

Any tips for couples on a tight wedding budget?

Decide on a nice, simple menu and price and stick to it. Don't let the cater bully you into spending more than you budgeted for.

Any decadent ideas for those with a lot to spend?

I guess if you really wanted to impress your guest you could go for a menu that would include hot and cold canapés, 3-5 courses, Amuse Bouche in between each course followed by cheese and port trolleys

What is the most important thing to remember when catering for a wedding?

The food!

What is your favourite wedding meal?

For me it would have to be a good charcuterie selection along with some nice local cheeses and freshly baked bread. Can't get much better than that in my opinion!

Thank you Alex.

Think about what you want to do with the leftovers. You can give them to the homeless, a charity or ask the caterer to box them up so guests can take them home.

Making Your Entrance

Typically your guests will go and sit down in the room where the wedding breakfast is situated. You will then be announced when everyone is seated. Everyone will stand and applaud until you are seated. It can be a little daunting if you are shy but we got caught up in the moment and it was a wonderful experience, all of our friends and family there, about to celebrate our first married meal with us.

For a personal touch, have a member of your family or someone that everyone will know announce you.

Make sure your photographer captures this moment. One of my favourite pictures from my wedding is a picture of my husband and I as we walk into the room, our faces the very encapsulation of happiness. It was taken by my father-in-law Michael. He captured the moment perfectly.

Getting The Cost Down

Table Planning

The seating plan is one of the hardest things about weddings. Especially when it comes to divorced families. It will cause many sleepless nights but don't let it get you down too much. Everyone should be on their best behaviour and act like an adult. At the end of the day, it is your day, not theirs so they should respect your decisions and take it with grace and a smile.

CHAPTER 17: PHOTOGRAPHER

Photography is very important. Why spend all of that money and not have a record of the day? Seems silly to me.

Choosing a wedding photographer can be terrifying. Wedding pictures hold a lot of emotions and they won't just be something that you look at for the rest of your life but also something that your grandchildren will look at. Their significance is not to be undervalued.

That doesn't mean, however, that you should let a photographer charge you an extortionate rate. Don't be afraid to negotiate and make sure that you know what you are getting before you pay the deposit. Most will give a discount of 15-20%. If they have gotten to an interview with you then they will want your business rather than having you go somewhere else. Don't be scared to hire a student. As long as they have a good portfolio, are reliable and have some good recommendations, you could save yourself a small fortune.

If you have a friend who is a photographer it is not necessarily a bad idea to have them do your wedding, as long as you are 100% confident that they will actually do the job and do it well. We asked a family friend to be our evening photographer and they completely forgot, we were devastated. Especially as we had to leave our wedding early. Just make sure your friend is talented, reliable and trustworthy. Not everyone can handle the pressure or get the job done.

It is a good idea for your photographer and videographer to see the venue beforehand. The consultation will ideally be done there. If not then they should arrive early on the day and also talk to the venue manager beforehand. A good photographer will want to see the venue beforehand so they know what they are doing on the day. They should not spend time on the day thinking about setting up shots and checking out the venue unless they do it before the hours they are booked for. If you are getting married in a church ask them for their rules about photography. They may not allow certain photography.

You will get a consultation with your photographer and when you do make sure you are firm about what you want. If they want to take you somewhere to do a specific shot and you are less keen then say so. Make sure you get along with your wedding photographer. They will be with you on the most important day of your life and you need to be able to relax in front of them. You will also need to be able to trust them. After the wedding you will also have to go through the pictures with them. Trust and security is important. Make sure you like their style too. Hire a photographer who shares your taste. Also make sure you get recommendations. Make sure that your photographer will supply high-resolution images. This one is important. You won't be able to share them or print them if they are not hi-res.

Things to watch out for from your photographer: do they seem jaded?

Are all of the pictures on their website of a consistent high-quality?
Do they badmouth past clients?
Do they actually like weddings?
What will they be shooting on?
What is the total price?
How many pictures will you get?
How many will be edited?
What format will you get your pictures on?
Do they have any back up equipment?
Are there any extra costs?
Do they shoot in colour or black and white?
Who will own the copyright?

Not all wedding photographers will be willing to give you all of your pictures so they can then protect their image. If this is important to you, ask them and then decide accordingly. However, do ask how many pictures you will get. This is important, some may give you only a small number that have been edited. Also ask about copyright. Some photographers retain copyright to your pictures even though they give you a disc. Sort this out beforehand as afterwards you will have less power. Sign a detailed contract stipulating what you want. Read carefully before signing on the dotted line. Make sure your wedding photographer is good at collaborating. They should be open to your ideas, not just adamant that their ideas are better.

Treat your photographer well and if they are going to be there all day then make sure there is some food for them. Even if it is just a sandwich. A good photographer will be unobtrusive, friendly and helpful on the day. They will manage people and calm them down.

When the wedding photographer is doing their job be firm with family members about taking their own pictures. You are paying a lot of money for a professional photographer and even if family members are professionals it is not really fair of them to barge in on something you are paying good money for. Their flash could also ruin some of the photographer's shots. Tell them, politely, to take their pictures when the photographer is finished. Don't take no for an answer.

To find a good wedding photographer ask any married couples you know, ask your wedding suppliers for any recommendations, ask on your social media network, look through bridal magazines, check out the suppliers section on wedding blogs and magazines and look at the real life weddings in wedding blogs and magazines.

Typing 'photographer + your location' into a search engine is a good way to find a wedding photographer. Or the previously mentioned hitched.co.uk. I met my amazing wedding photographer Emma-Jane at a press day and my (then) fiancé loved her work. She has an amazing eye.

Another thing to look out for is testimonials. Many photographers will have some on their website and others will give them on demand.

When it comes to a wedding package, they usually charge in sets of hours. We had our photographer for three hours and in the time she got a lot of very good shots.

Be careful if you hire a family member to do your photography. They may be brilliant at what they do but they also might get drunk, distracted or not want to take pictures all night. Photography is something that is worth investing in.

Choosing a Style

All photographers have a specific style. Make sure your photographer suits your style and the tone you want for the day. Also think about what kind of editing you want. You might want something more natural so then don't hire a photographer who is obsessed with Photoshop and crazy effects. If you like their pictures but not their style of editing the relationship might not work. Hire someone who has everything you want all in one.

Making a Shot List

It is easier to make a shot list on the day and then hand it to your maid of honour or best man. They can then round people up and make the process faster. Many people will get restless if the photography goes on too long. It is also a good idea to get the group shots out of the way and then the bride and groom go off somewhere close but secluded to get the couple shots done.

Some ideas for your shot list. It will help to have their actual names, not just their roles and give the shot list to the best man or maid of honour.

Bride with father.
Bride with parents.
Bride with grandparents.
Bride with family.
Bride with bridesmaids.
Groom with mother.
Groom with parents.
Groom with best man.
Groom with ushers.
Group shot.

Fees and packages

Think hard about the package you want. Wedding photography is incredibly expensive. Most, if not all, wedding photographers will offer a range of different packages. You might not be able to afford the entire day to be done but in the age of social media and iPhones your guests will probably take some amazing pictures anyway. The best time to have a photographer is for the first three hours. This will cover: getting ready, the ceremony and the reception. No one really wants their picture taken when they are eating but you could ask people to take pictures of the speeches and the dancing.

If you have the money then go all out and hire them for the entire day. Just make sure that you feed them or that they know in advance there won't be any food. I understand wedding catering is expensive and charges per head but you don't want your photographer fainting from hunger or going out to get something to eat and missing an important moment. Some photographers will ask for some sandwiches or something. I think this is a reasonable request and your caterer should not mind if it is just one or two. You will probably have bread there on the day anyway. If your caterer will charge you extra then factor this in however. Photographers are expensive and so is wedding catering. When you are paying a premium for both any added extras can be a bit much.

Choosing Which Pictures

You will probably have to choose a limited number of pictures that will get edited but should get all of the pictures on a disc. Make sure your photographer will give you all of the pictures before you book them. You might get your pictures as a contact sheet (especially if the photographer used a camera that was not digital), an internet album or print. They will not be edited at first but will be the raws, i.e the footage straight from the camera. Many photographers will lightly edit their raws before showing them to you.

Choosing what pictures you want can be difficult and exhausting. There will probably be hundreds on the contact sheet and they may even start blurring into one. Choose the pictures that grab you first and if you are only allowed a certain amount of pictures then think carefully before you ask family members if they want any as they might get disappointed if you have to sacrifice a few. If they can buy their own and are willing to then this should not be a problem however.

Wedding Album

Some photographers do add-ons like wedding albums or heart-shaped USB keys. Buy them if you like them or get them cheaper on eBay if money is tight.

An investment you may want to make, or even better, put one on your gift list, is a good photo frame to display your wedding photo. We got very lucky and won a beautiful Vera Wang photo frame at a Peter Jones wedding gift list event. Your wedding day is (hopefully) one of the best days of your life so show it off in style.

Photography is very important. What is the point of spending so much money on your wedding if you don't have a record of it that stands the test of time? If you do not have a proper record of your day you will be disappointed. It will also be one of the few times when you have all of your friends and family in one place, do not let that opportunity go.

Our wedding photographer, **Emma from Emma-Jane**

Photography was absolutely amazing. We could not have asked for a better photographer. Our wedding photos are amazing and she really has a great eye. We will treasure our wedding pictures forever.

Emma is a stunningly talented photographer and she was amazing on the day. She made everyone relaxed and has an amazing eye for a good picture. She gave me an interview with lots of great advice in it.

Emma from Emma-Jane Photography.

What made you get into wedding photography?

I started off assisting and modelling with a photographer about five years ago now. I had an interest in the wedding side of being a photographer and then second shot a few other weddings before setting up as a freelancer. The process was fairly quick in my transition as I knew it was a market I could get into due to my fashion and conceptual background as a photographer.

What should couples look for in a wedding photographer?

Couples should start by identifying what sort of wedding photography style they like such as documentary, fashion or some photographers actually still shoot on film. It would then be about seeing what photographers are either within an area if they do not want to add on extra travel costs or who they could fly over. This would be a case of a photographer's work that they really love and then look to narrow a few of these down to meet with in person. The personal interaction will probably be the deciding factor as the couple will need to get on with their photographer as having them there is a very personal part of their day.

What kind of questions should a couple ask their wedding photographer?

Ideally this should be things such as how do they see the shots taking form? Do they have an assistant for very large weddings? What happens in regards to post production and the number of images that the couple will receive? Are there any wedding albums included in the packages, if not how much do these cost if needed after the day? What kit does the photographer use? As you want to see they are using full format cameras, good lenses and have back-ups on the day.

How is wedding photography different from normal photography?

As a wedding photographer this does differ more in the way that everything is at a much faster pace for the photographer to keep track of. The photographer has to

have very good communication with the couple beforehand at the consultations so that the plan of the days shots are outlined even if this differs slightly on the day.

The photographer will need to be experienced, with a minimum of 6/7 solo weddings under their belt in my opinion before the competency is there. There is also a lot more communication and post-production of the event compared to family or commercial photography.

What is the most important thing to capture on the day?

Everything is equally important, it is about documenting the day itself and giving the whole day as a reminder and people getting that feeling back. For me the bits that seem to be at the top of my list are the look the groom has before the ceremony, the first kiss, and the couple shots away from the party after the ceremony.

Talk us through your working day during a wedding.

Night before preparation of kit
Morning, double check kit
Travel and arrive at wedding
Getting ready shots
Documentation shots
Integrating myself as part of the wedding party
Arrival at church or location
Chat with registrar or vicar to make sure they are still ok with images and where not to stand to stop invasion of service
Document ceremony
Couple shots separate away from wedding party
Wedding shots of guests
Documenting interactions
Cake and detail shots
Speeches
Cake cutting
First dance

Each couple's wedding is different but this is a bit more standard for a full day's shoot.

What if someone doesn't like having their picture taken, any tips?

This is always tricky and will depend on who they are in the wedding party, if it is a guest they are a little less of your focus so you do your best to relax them but they are not the sole focus, the couple are. If it is the bride or groom though, this does pose a problem. In the past I have had an engagement shoot with them to relax and get them used to the camera and my way of working. And then talk them through each step during the day itself, joke, have fun and try to make it easy.

What is your favourite thing about doing wedding photography?

As I am a fashion photographer I tend to like the stylised shots the best, so the details and dress, and the couple shots after the ceremony where you can play with background and dynamics of the shots.

Have you spotted any trends?

There have been a few trends of having more of an 'instagramed' feel for the post-production and also eco type weddings, with hand-made decorations and a very country type feel.

You have a very good eye, any tips for couples who want to be original in their wedding photography?

Do your research. You need to figure out what it is you like, if you like traditional you will find it hard getting out of that box. But if you are open to your wedding photographer being creative chat through what is available: any props or great settings at the locations so you can create a dramatic backdrop.

How do you choose where to take pictures? How important is location?

Location is the most important thing for me. This means I need good lighting and ideally a good backdrop to take the couple away for after the ceremony so that some nice private shots are done as these are the shots they will most likely use. If you have a small venue and no outside location you are really limiting your photographer and the shots.

Any other tips and advice?

Make sure that communication is key on both sides. You need to know what is expected of your photographer and equally your photographer needs to know what you want in regards to shots, any changes and last minute things before the day. As well as being open during the day itself to changes and any new ideas.

Thank you Emma.

It is a good idea to print out a copy or two of your wedding photos. My husband and I have them on USB and on each of our computers but a print copy is a great idea just in case. It also means you can frame some. There are companies that will print your wedding photos for you and then send them to you in a nice album. This can be done inexpensively. If you have a good colour printer you could print them out yourself on some photo paper. I do this with pictures and they look just as good as if they were done professionally.

If you are worried about how your chin will look in pictures then look up. Not all the way, but slightly in all of the pictures. If you are worried about your arms then don't hold them too close to your body. Having your elbows at an angle will make them look slimmer.

Videographer

This is another thing that I would not have gone without. We love our wedding video and it is so wonderful to have a record of the day. Our videographer, **Kevin from Federated Films** was truly amazing. He even had the wedding video done in just over a week. Very impressive. I interviewed him for this book and he gave me some great answers.

Here is his biography: While Kevin was still at University in 1984, he made his first ever short film; it was a 5 minute computer-generated story created by programming graphics on a BBC Micro and recording it frame-by-frame on a domestic video recorder. After winning a national competition with the film he got a job in the newly emerging field of digital media in the late 80s and he has been creating films and exploring using technology to communicate ideas and stories ever since. In 2006 Kevin went on to master his craft by studying film making at Brighton Film School and London's Raindance Film School as well as at the BBC.

How did you get into wedding videography?

I shot a few friends' weddings over the years as wedding gifts and they were always thrilled with the results and though my main focus is shooting corporate films I do enjoy capturing that special day for a new couple to look back on.

Tell us about your process when doing weddings?

It's important to get a feel for what style of shooting the bride and groom want. Capturing video is more intrusive than taking photographers as you get to hear what people are saying as well as doing. I try to be as unobtrusive as possible but also still get into the middle of the action to capture the important moments.

What should people consider when choosing a videographer?

Well firstly do you share the same vision for what you want to capture on the day? The video should be shot in High Definition and preferably with a Digital SLR camera as they capture so much more light and colour especially in low light situations.

What is the most important thing in wedding videography?

Capturing the emotions of the day, it's not about the flowers or the cake, though they are important, it's about people expressing their joy as well as a few tears. I shoot at double frame rate so I can slow down these moments to heighten the drama.

Is a videographer essential?

Of course we can all shoot video on our phones and even our stills cameras these days, but the most important aspect of a good video is the sound, if you can't hear what people are saying then it makes a video hard to watch. I use radio microphones and broadcast quality boom mikes to capture the sound at the highest quality.

What kind of questions should people ask their videographer?

Well, ask to see their last video, does it capture the moment and create an emotional connection with the bride and groom, if it does then hire them but if it's all shots of flowers, cars and cakes then a good stills photographer can capture that.

What is the most important moment to capture?

The bride walking down the aisle, the look of love between the bride and groom when they say their vows, interviews with the families, the first dance and everyone else's dancing and finally the drive off into the sunset of the newly married couple.

Tell us about some of the weddings you have done?

Well I've done ballrooms, barns and even a rowing club, but no churches yet!

What is the most important thing you have learned about filming weddings?

Befriend the wedding planner and the photographer – they can help you capture the best moments of the day.

Are you a fan of weddings?

It's great to see two families meeting for the first time and feeling all the love in the room and best wishes for two people's future together.

What is your favourite part of filming weddings?

Delivering the final film and getting the call that says they love it and it made them cry.

And the least?

Well, you shoot a lot of material and it takes a long time to go through all the rushes to find the special moments, but it is the foundation work you need to do to create a great wedding video.

Thank you Kevin.

It is a good idea to find out what your videographer will be filming on. Also find out what format you will get your wedding video on. Some will give a DVD and others will send you a link to download the video. Before you book your videographer check out their other wedding videos. Make sure they are in focus, tell the story and capture all of the moments. Make sure the videos are well edited. Another thing to watch out for is sound. If the sound is bad then go for another videographer. It is very important. There should be a microphone near the bride or groom when they are doing their vows. A mic pinned onto the groom is usually the best way.

You will want some music on your video. It would be quite dull without it. There are plenty of sites out there that do royalty-free music. Just type 'royalty-free music' into a search engine. Give your photographer and videographer each other's details. That way you can have some of your wedding pictures in the video. It really adds something and breaks up the video nicely.

As ever: ask for a discount. Especially if you are getting married off-peak. Ask them how long it will take them to edit the video. It may take a while for them to edit the video but they still have an obligation to get it to you in a reasonable amount of time.

It has become popular in recent years to hire equipment from companies that then take the footage and edit if for you. Shoot It Yourself is a popular one. My husband actually thought about doing our own videography because we have all of the equipment to do so. However, I didn't want the stress or the hassle. Despite that, if you have some friends or cousins who would be up for filming the wedding then this can be a cheaper option. Not many people are good at filming or will have a steady hand so choose the people carefully. Shoot It Yourself packages start at £849 which is not cheap. Another thing to think about is if guests will be happy 'working' at your wedding. Some won't mind and it could even be your wedding present. The best thing is to allocate certain people different time slots. Make sure that they don't get drunk when on duty and that they use a tripod to keep the camera steady. It is best if they don't try any fancy techniques: panning, zooming etc. Having guests make speeches to the camera is a nice touch. As is capturing the entire day from start to finish. The more footage you have to work with, the better the video will be.

CHAPTER 18: HONEYMOON

Possibly the most fun part of weddings. The part where you and your new husband are alone in a fun destination, well, you will have champagne to keep you company but otherwise it is just you and your new spouse. The honeymoon is so called because the first month of marriage is supposed to be the sweetest. It is also a well-deserved break after the stress of planning a wedding. The honeymoon will require budgeting and planning just like the wedding did, but the true beauty of it is that there is only you and your spouse to please. That does not mean it will be easy however. My husband and I could not agree on where to have our honeymoon, we just wanted to go to different places. In the end either one of you or both of you may have to compromise.

Cutting the cost

Book as far in advance as you can, this will save you money. It will also help to make sure people know you are newlyweds. You should at least get some free champagne.

Deciding Where To Go

A sit down to decide where you both want to go is the best way to get things started. You may both have ideas of where you want to go or you might want to get some travel magazines or go on the internet. Decide what type of honeymoon you want and what will suit your personalities. Are you both active or do you just want a beach holiday? Will you want lots of activities and things to see and do or just a nice, relaxing time with a cocktail in hand? Do you want to be hot or cold? If you decide what type of honeymoon you want it will be much easier to decide where to go.

The next key thing to think about is seasons. If you have a travel agent then they will know when to go where. If not then it is time to research on the internet.

Where to go when:

January

South Africa, Chile, India, Burma, Australia, Kenya, Cambodia, Thailand, Barbados, Maldives, Venezuela, Bangladesh, Canada, New Mexico, Belize, Hawaii, Tahiti, New Zealand, Laos, Jamaica, Costa Rica, Hong Kong, Peru, Philippines, Spain, Ivory Coast or Nigeria.

February

Morocco, Marrakech, Atlas Mountains, Canary Islands, Tenerife, Lanzarote, Gran Canaria, Oman, Dubai, Jordan, The Gambia, Caribbean, Cuba, Venice, Egypt,

Northern India, Vietnam, Burma, Malaysia, Bali, Galapagos Islands, Australia, New Zealand, Moscow, Colorado, Norway, New York, Chicago, Las Vegas, Utah, Miami.

March

South Korea, Japan, Miami, Cape Town, Manila, Maldives, Malaysia, Mexico, Berlin, Panama, Costa Rica, Western Australia, California, Hong Kong, Ireland, France, Austria, Tuscany, Rome, Barcelona, Cuba, Guatemala, Nepal, Sri Lanka, the Alps, Argentina, Florida.

April

Phoenix (USA), Bombay, Malta, Tunisia, Lebanon, Libya, Death Valley (USA), Greece, Vietnam, Australia, Guatemala, Nepal, Vietnam, Crete, Costa Rica, South Africa, Philippines, Maldives, Peru, Venezuela, Cuba, Algeria, Spain, Madagascar, Barbados, Jamaica, Bahamas, Portugal, Honolulu, Turkey, Namibia, Zimbabwe, Botswana, Cape Verde, Yemen, Oman, Senegal, Egypt, Mauritania.

May

Jordan, Cyprus, Turkey, Lebanon, Egypt, Portugal, Israel, Phoenix (USA), Malta, Uzbekistan, Tunisia, Honolulu, Bombay, Spain, Russia, Cape Verde, Greece, Morocco, Beijing, Los Angeles, Morocco, Italy, Albania, Australia, Azerbaijan, Algeria, Barbados, Crete, Rome, Angola, South Africa, Brazil, Peru, Vietnam, Burundi, Angola, Madagascar.

June

Israel, Jordan, Peru, Spain, Brazil, Kenya, Angola, Netherlands, France, Reunion (Saint-Denis), Mauritius, London, Tanzania, Burundi, India, South Africa, Austria, Poland, Germany, Cape Verde, Italy, Spain, China, Canada, Hungary, Slovak Republic, Algeria, Australia, Portugal, Russia, Greece, Morocco, Albania, Greece, Los Angeles, Honolulu, Tunisia, Turkey, Armenia, Croatia, Mauritania.

July

Jordan, Crete, Israel, Uzbekistan, Turkey, Greece, Beirut, Croatia, Malta, Portugal, Spain, Tunisia, Los Angeles, France, Italy, Albania, Romania, Honolulu, Morocco, Russia, Azerbaijan, Algeria, Andorra, Hungary, Geneva, Bulgaria, Sweden, Seattle, San Francisco, Barcelona, The Alps, Venice, Palmero, Naples, Belarus, Australia, Finland, Mauritania, Vancouver, China, Burundi, Prague, Brazil, Tanzania, Indonesia, Mauritius, Cape Verde, French Polynesia, London, Germany, York (UK), Togo, Peru, Angola.

August

Ivory Coast, Peru, Nigeria, Detroit, San Francisco, Benin, Togo, Netherlands, London, Angola, New Caledonia, French Polynesia, South Africa, Seychelles, Warsaw, Brazil, Reunion (Saint-Denis), Paris, Mauritius, Rio de Janeiro, Denmark, Berlin, Burundi, Indonesia, Venice, India, Seattle, Toronto, Ottawa, Prague, Vancouver, China, Spain, Jakarta, Russia, Palermo, The Alps, Budapest, Tanzania, Bratislava, Darwin, Morocco, Bulgaria, Rome, Muscat, Bucharest, Algeria, Madrid, Azerbaijan, Madrid, Los Angeles, Honolulu, Armenia, Albania, Tunisia, Istanbul, Lisbon, Beirut.

September

Jordan, Jerusalem, Cyprus, Turkey, Botswana, Zimbabwe, Crete, Cairo, Marrakesh, Namibia, Los Angeles, Izmir, Bodrum. Greece, Tunisia, Darwin, Athens, Armenia, Baku, Beirut, Guyana, Malta, Lisbon, Madrid, Dallas, San Francisco, Corsica, Honolulu, Morocco, Spain, Portugal, Albania, Algeria, Istanbul, Jakarta, Beijing, Mauritius, Rome, Reunion (Saint-Denis), India, France, Greece, Naples, Brazil, Sardinia, Brisbane, Bali, French Polynesia, Bratislava, Budapest, Venice, Noumea (New Caledonia), Togo, Burundi, Paris, Milan, Benin, Rio de Janeiro, Peru, Angola.

October

Jordan, Zimbabwe, Nepal, Yemen, Namibia, Phoenix (USA), Death Valley (USA), Alice Springs, Madagascar, Cayenne, Dar es Salaam, Botswana, Cairo, Cyprus, Mauritania, Johannesburg, Reunion (Saint-Denis), Port-Louise, Pretoria, Los Angeles, Turkey, Brazil, New Caledonia, Beirut, Marrakesh, Port Elizabeth, Bombay, San Francisco, Honolulu, Morocco, Tunisia, Portugal, Brisbane, Cape Verde, Azerbaijan, Athens, Jerusalem, Lisbon, Malta, Togo, Kenya, Atlanta, Crete, Aegean Islands, Peru, China, Angola, Burundi, Lima.

November

Cape town, Sanaa, Muscat, Namibia, India, Senegal, Port-Louis, Mauritania, Reunion (Saint-Denis), Port Elizabeth, Bombay, Hyderabad, Brazil, Benin, Botswana, Cairo, Lome, Laos, Calcutta, Adelaide, Bangkok, Chiang Mai, Praia, Noumea (New Caledonia), Bangladesh, Nigeria, Hong Kong, Turkey, Belem, Nicaragua, Almeria, Honolulu, Las Palmas, Portugal, Athens, Wuzhou, Lima, Guatemala, Hanoi, Crete, Naxos, Aegean Islands.

December

Havana, Bombay, Sanaa (Yemen), Canberra, Cape Town, Namibia, India, Oman, Cambodia, South Africa, Port Elizabeth, Adelaide, Bangkok, Chiang Mai, Bangladesh, Mali, Senegal, Togo, Mauritania, Laos, Calcutta, Burma, Brazil, Jamaica, Caracas, Noumea (New Caledonia), Benin, Lagos, Miami, Melbourne, Bahamas, Praia (Cape Verde), Burma, Costa Rica, Spain, Hong Kong, Nicaragua,

Angola, Guatemala, Havana, Peru, Dominican Republic, China: Wuzhou, Ho Chi Ming City, Hanoi.

There are some good ideas there and it by no means covers every destination. Before you choose a destination you should not only check the weather, but also rumours of political upheaval. You don't want to spend your honeymoon in the mists of a civil war.

These are some of the most popular honeymoon destinations.

Mexico
Italy
Fiji
South Africa
Tanzania
Seychelles
Bahamas
Florlda
Maldives
Aruba

If you do book a honeymoon with a lot of physical activities then make sure you have a few days where you can just relax and do nothing. Planning a wedding is exhausting and when it is over you will be completely exhausted and experiencing a major comedown. Give yourself some time to recover and your body and mental health will thank you later. Also make sure you are physically up to any excursions you may have planned. You may be married now but if you couldn't climb mountains before, you can't do it now.

Another good tip is to keep away from anywhere that holds bad memories and anywhere that you went with an ex. You don't need ghosts or bad memories hanging around your honeymoon.

Bringing The Family

If you already have children you might want to bring them. There are no rules. Do so if you want. You could leave them with a family member of course and celebrate your honeymoon just the two of you. If you do end up bringing your children then check for childcare facilities at the hotel.

If you are a couple who have been married before and are bringing children to the relationship then a familymoon will be a great way for the family to get to know one another and get used to living in the same space. It can be a good introduction into the new family scenario. It is also a good idea to plan a trip where children can have some time on their own. Camping may be too much, especially if you have teenagers. A resort or a cruise with adjoining rooms is a good idea. Make sure each child gets some time with you and your new spouse but that you also have some time alone. Make sure no one feels excluded. Keep everyone's different interests in mind, you want there to be something for everyone. Don't push the children into doing anything or liking each other. Just let everyone get to know each other on their own terms.

You can try and take a proper honeymoon after the familymoon if you can. Even if it is just a minimoon (a mini honeymoon).

Travel Agent

They are worth a try. They know their stuff and might be able to get you a good deal. You could also include a honeymoon option on your gift list.

Secret Escapes

Secret Escapes is a great site with a lot of great travel deals. They tend to give good discounts. We booked our minimoon to Langshott Manor in Surrey through them. We got a good deal and we had a lot of fun.

Researching

The internet is an amazing resource. It will have a ton of information and even just typing 'honeymoon' into a search engine will give you a good amount of ideas and options.

Bridal magazines are also a great source of information and have a lot of recourses and links. Be sure to check out their websites too.

The internet allows you to be your own travel agent. There are many discount travel sites and lots of great deals available. There will also be customer reviews online which will make sure you don't get scammed. Also check the company you want to book with on watchdog sites. You could also check that they are with ABTA, ABTA makes sure that companies adhere to a strict code of conduct. This ensures a high standard.

You can also use the internet to make sure you are getting the cheapest deal on your flight and hotel booking. There are also many comparison sites on which you can check all of the different flight prices against each other.

In some cases the man would plan the entire honeymoon as a surprise for the bride. This is because the bride generally planned the wedding. You could still do this of course. A surprise honeymoon will delight many brides and I asked my husband to do this for me as I planned our entire wedding and was just sick of planning. If you have done all of the wedding, it is only fair that the groom pulls his weight in some way. If you planned the wedding together however then also planning the honeymoon together is fair and can also be fun.

Choosing a Travel Agent

While travel agents do take commission, working with one might also save you money in the long run. They are very knowledgeable and have good contacts. Just make sure you know what you want and don't get bullied into spending more money than you are comfortable with, or going somewhere that your heart is not set on.

Give the travel agent some options and then ask them what they recommend. Ask the travel agent if they have been there personally. Check that, if something goes wrong, they can help and you won't just be stranded. Asking for contact details or a contact person/phone number is a good idea. Ask them what kind of deals they can do for you, if they have specific honeymoon packages and what kind of discount they can get you. Bargain hard and don't be embarrassed to negotiate. Check if they work in conjunction with the tour operators and how quickly they will return your phone calls. Will they help you with visas, passports, any immunisations or documents that you will need? Ask them when you will receive all of your tickets and documentations, make sure that you will get them on time. It is also a good idea to enquire if you can get any references or testimonials from other couples who had their honeymoon planned by the agent. This would be even better if the couple are going to the same place and have the same budget as you. Ask them if they have any videos or literature that you can look at. You want to know what your hotel looks like and exactly where you will be staying. Ask if the pictures and information are up-to-date. It won't be fun if you get there and there is now a building site next to your hotel. It also helps if the agent in particular specialises in the area where you want to go. Ask friends and people on the internet for recommendations on specific agents, instead of an agency.

Here are some tips on saving money:

Rent a house instead of staying in a hotel.

Renting a home can be surprisingly cheap. Hotels can be very expensive and there are usually extra service charges. You can also buy your own food and alcohol if you stay in a private home. It can be cheaper still if you book off-peak.

Register for a honeymoon fund rather than a gift list.

Most of us already have far too many things. More clutter is usually not needed and buying more things is not good for the environment. Instead of making a list of things you want you can register for a honeymoon fund instead. Plenty of sites like Prezola allow you to create a honeymoon fund, giving guests the option of paying for a honeymoon meal, a flight upgrade or some champagne. Even if you register with Debenhams or John Lewis there will be an option to include a honeymoon fund. The catch is that you must do it with their travel agent. For John Lewis this is Kuoni and for Debenhams it is Virgin Holidays.

Putting 'the couple prefer honeymoon contributions to gifts' on your invite lets people know your preference. Don't worry if some guests don't like it or make comments, it is much wiser financially and better for the environment than accumulating more stuff. Let them be stuffy about it.

Go off-peak. Having a honeymoon in July or August is bound to be expensive. This may mean delaying your honeymoon but it will be worth it if you can save a lot of money.

Get travel insurance. This can save you a substantial amount of money if something goes wrong.

Make sure everything is legit. Book with a reputable travel agent or travel website. Watch out for scams.

Get a competitive deal when exchanging currency. Shop around and don't just accept the first deal you get. Check with your bank on how much they charge for cash withdrawals when you are abroad. Find out the cheapest and easiest way to get your hands on your own money.

Always ask if the price includes VAT. VAT really does add a lot on top. Also check for other taxes and service charges.

Use Student Discounts

Avoid the minibar. Even better, ask the hotel to remove everything from it and then put your own stuff in. Try to avoid room service too, it is usually horrendously expensive.

Book in advance. Booking in advance will always help to keep costs down.

Make sure you pack enough stuff so you don't need to buy anything when on holiday.

Take a copy of your marriage certificate with you. Many hotels and resorts will give some added extras or discounts for newlyweds. Most do this so you will keep coming back. Take a copy, not the original document.

Use any air miles you have. Join a frequent flyer club and gain benefits.

Some **youth hostels** have private rooms which will be cheaper than a hotel and, hopefully, nice enough for a stay.

Think carefully before you go all-inclusive. It might be cheaper not to do so.

Dropping hints that you just got married might also end up in some perks. Don't be loud about it but a few subtle comments might make a difference.

Perfect Planning Tips

Before you go make sure you have an up-to-date passport in the correct name (change your name after or before the wedding). Many countries require that you have at least six months left on your passport for entry. All of the vaccinations that are needed, visas and some countries require HIV/AIDS testing. Check this first. The Foreign Office www.gov.uk/foreign-travel-advice should help you with anything you need to know.

If you are renting a car then try and prepay through a travel agent. Prices can fluctuate. Making sure the tank is full when you return it is also usually a good idea as it is cheaper than paying the hire company's per-gallon charge.

Remember that in America you have to be twenty-five to rent a car with a lot of the big companies. Alamo will rent to drivers between twenty-one and twenty-four for an extra $20 per day. Unfair but worth noting. If you are younger then seeking out a smaller, little-known hire company will probably save you money.

What To Pack

Have your luggage sent to the hotel or at least make sure it is in the boot of the car. If you are leaving for your honeymoon straight away then give your outfits to a member of the wedding party or a family member to be dry-cleaned/returned to the rental shop.

Honeymoon clothes.
Hairdryer.
Insect repellent.
Some sexy underwear. It is your honeymoon after all.
Sun lotion.
After Sun.
Bottle Opener.
Camera and camera battery and charger.
Contraceptive. Unless you are trying to conceive.
Passports.
Drivers licence.
Earplugs.
Adapter.
Hats.
Tablets for indigestion, diarrhoea and other possible ailments. Also include plasters and painkillers.
Sandals.
Music.
Manicure set.
All of your tickets.
Vitamins.
Torch.

Mini sewing kit.
A travel pillow.

You might also want to bring a sealable plastic bag as you will probably have to put your toiletries into one and some airports now try to charge you £1 for one. Daylight robbery.

CHAPTER 19: TIPS FOR CUTTING COSTS

Tips For Saving Money

Cutting the guest list.

This is the best and easiest way to cut the budget. Every single person who comes to your wedding costs you money. So be ruthless and don't feel you have to give everyone a plus one. Cutting children from your wedding will also save money but if you do this make it a rule across the board. If some guests have gone to the expense of hiring a babysitter and then see other children running around they are probably not going to be happy about it.

Cut the hours

The longer the wedding the more it will cost to feed people and give them drinks. You don't have to have a long wedding, just do whatever you want. This will be easier if you have to be out of the venue at a set time but don't feel like you have to use all of your allocated time, or pay to entertain your guests for the full amount of time. As long as you feed people and give them a certain amount of alcohol then they should be grateful and not too bothered if they have to put their hand in their pocket at the end of the night.

Marry off-peak

Getting married during the week will save money not only on the venue, but also with suppliers too. Your guests will have to take a day off work so factor this in. An autumn or winter wedding will also be cheaper.

Online

Buy things cheaply online and also check for cheaper deals than you have been offered. Car boot sales and charity shops will also have cheap stuff that could come in handy.

Getting Organised

Being organised and booking things in advance will save lots of money.

Minimoon

This is a mini honeymoon that couples have when they have to delay their honeymoon. You can also extend your first night hotel stay into a mini honeymoon. Staycations are best for minimoons. There are plenty of amazing places in the United Kingdom where you can have a romantic getaway. Cornwall, Brighton, Scotland, Wales, Ireland, Devon, London…the possibilities are endless.

Have Your Honeymoon in Europe

If you live in the United Kingdom then not only will having a honeymoon in Europe be easy to get to, it will also be a lot cheaper. There are plenty of beautiful, romantic places to go.

Have Prosecco Instead of Champagne.

It is cheaper but tastes just as good. As long as you buy the right one.

CHAPTER 20: OTHER TIPS AND HINTS

I got wedding planner Mariella Kamburova to write about her top wedding planning tips if you and your future spouse are from different cultures to help you on your way.

I am an experienced wedding planner based in London, UK, and have been running my highly successful and well known business in Bulgaria since 2004.

Being the first graduate wedding planner in my country, I have been fortunate enough to plan weddings and family events for many celebrities, politicians and respected business people from all over the world. I am happy to say that my experience is an excellent source of useful tips for brides to be.

Today I'd love to share with you 7 ways how you can mix and match two different nationalities and cultures which mean differing traditions and rituals from two countries.

My passion is to find the most interesting and comparable traditions or symbolic references from two different countries and to create an extraordinary event, has always been one of the most inspiring tasks in my line of work.

If you and your hubby to be are from two different cultures, here are my tips how to create your magical and unforgettable wedding day:

1. Start with making a list of all traditions and rituals which both countries have. In two columns, write everything you know as traditions from each country. In column "A" you write all traditions from your country and in column "B" write all traditions of your fiancé's country.
Putting everything together on a piece of paper will give you a complete overview and will help you to pick those traditions which you both like and will suit you most.

2. Choose as many traditions and rituals as you'd like to have, however, try to mix and match them nicely to provide a good balance.
Apart from the first dance, cutting the wedding cake and bouquet toss, there are so many other funny or even weird traditions and rituals that can be found. From waving with white napkins to welcoming the newlywed in Belgium to beating the feet of the groom in Korea, kidnapping the bride in Romania, Polterabend – smashing dishes – in Germany, or throwing peas instead of rice over newlyweds in the Czech Republic … Every country has its own unique traditions.

   However, to be interesting and enjoyable for you and your guests, avoid having two or more traditions at the same time. Spread them evenly during the day and the evening in your wedding day programme. In addition, it will be very helpful if your DJ, for instance, makes a short introductory explanation at the start of each tradition, so that your guests will have an understanding of the tradition occurring.

3. Some countries have traditional symbols, therefore you can decide to implement these as a decorative element into your wedding.
   Think about those symbols and elements in a creative way – how and where you can have them. Stationery, guest tables, the theme of the centrepieces and flowers or wedding cake... Could be a wonderful idea to implement them as special elements of your ceremony, for instance, if one of the countries is popular with wine production you may use cask wine for the altar table and have the wedding toast with glass of wine. Then, if in the other country breaking the glass is a good symbol, you can break the glasses immediately after the toast to honour the tradition.

4. Colours:
   Colours are an integral part of the traditions and no doubt the colours will be a very important part of the wedding. If there are not many traditions and elements which you are willing to mix, why don't you think about the colours of your national flags. Small ribbons for guests' favours with the colours of your flags, candles with the same colours or even the bridesmaids' dresses are all beautiful elements with which you can personalise your wedding day.

5. Food and drinks:
   You can expand the experience of the taste of both countries by using significant recipes of traditional cuisines. Two buffets with a piece of traditional food-based delights and delicious drinks will be a wonderful touch. Small bottles of traditional drinks could be great favours for your guests like liquors, whisky or port wine.

6. Entertainment:
   One of the strongest and most remarkable ways to mix two cultures is in the entertainment. Dancers and/or singers during the evening, hostesses dressed in traditional clothing or attractive musical instruments for your ceremony. The waiting staff also can be included by having uniforms with traditional elements.

7. Wedding cake and guest book:
   The wedding cake is one of my favourite elements of the wedding. I love to discuss the design of the cake with my clients and together to create something unique and unforgettable. The wedding cake, as a symbol of the sweet part of the marriage, is intended to be a very special element of your wedding, therefore you should pay special attention to this detail. If you'd like to have place where you display your wedding cake, you may choose to include a guest book which matches the design of the wedding cake. For instance, my clients had chosen a wedding cake with a world map on it with the idea to

mark both countries with hearts and to connect them with ribbon. I suggested next to the wedding cake to place a paper world map where all their guests were able to write their well wishes for them.

Have fun with planning your wedding and remember - the best time of your life is coming up!

Thank you, Mariella

What I Wish I Had Done Differently

Stayed local. Less stress and complications. Even having a supplier in another part of London can be stressful.

Been firmer with people who interfered or bullied. Wedding planning may be stressful and hard but it should still be a fun time and a once-in-a-lifetime experience. Don't let anyone ruin that for you.

Thought some of my decisions through before just saying yes or agreeing to something. Been firmer with suppliers I thought were rude or not up to par.

Been adamant about the stag do being at least two weeks before the wedding. Would have saved a lot of heartache.

Ignored people who were bitchy, rude or negative to me. Unfortunately, there will probably be some. Don't let them get to you. Hold on to positive people and things. If people have a problem then it is their problem, not yours.

Had some people attend the wedding who ended up not being there on the day.

Being too polite to some suppliers initially. Had to get tougher as some treat you like a friend, which is fine, as long as they also remember that you are a customer.

Started the DIY projects earlier. Doing the menus, seating plan and favours on the same day we had to buy the orange juice and drop everything off at the venue was not fun. Especially when we had to not only design and print the menus, but also cut them out of the card. It took ages as we had to do over 50 menus and we printed two on each piece of paper. Pretty dire.

Gone shopping with my bridesmaids for their dresses and made a day of it. Some afternoon tea or champagne afterwards would have been great too.

Blogs And Websites of Note

There are a lot of great websites and blogs out there for the modern bride. You don't have to buy a print magazine at all, although that is fun and there are plenty of good ones out there. I have listed just a few of the amazing websites and blogs out there. Have fun as the researching is often the most fun part.

http://www.hitched.co.uk

rocknrollbride.com

http://www.bridesmagazine.co.uk

marthastewartweddings.com

confetti.co.uk

CHAPTER 21: QUOTES ON MARRIAGE

The problem with marriage is that it ends every night after making love, and it must be re-built every morning before breakfast. – Gabriel García Márquez.

Believing in marriage and not in divorce is like believing in joint stock companies and not in bankruptcy. – Neil Ferguson

Marriage is a wonderful institution, but who wants to live in an institution? – Groucho Marx

Where there's marriage without love, there will be love without marriage. – Benjamin Franklin

If I get married, I want to be very married. – Audrey Hepburn

When you make the sacrifice in marriage, you're sacrificing not to each other but to unity in a relationship. – Joseph Campbell

When marrying, ask yourself this question: Do you believe that you will be able to con-verse well with this person into your old age? Everything else in marriage is transitory. – Friedrich Nietzsche

Every good relationship, especially marriage, is based on respect. If it's not based on re-spect, nothing that appears to be good will last very long. – Amy Grant

I love being married. It's so great to find that one special person you want to annoy for the rest of your life. – Rita Rudner

My most brilliant achievement was my ability to be able to persuade my wife to marry me. – Winston Churchill

Let the wife make the husband glad to come home, and let him make her sorry to see him leave.
- Martin Luther

Don't marry the person you think you can live with; marry only the individual you think you can't live without. – James C. Dobson

It is not a lack of love, but a lack of friendship that makes unhappy marriages. – Friedrich Nietzsche

Do you know what it means to come home at night to a woman who'll give you a little love, a little affection, a little tenderness? It means you're in the wrong house, that's what it means.- Henny Youngman

The Wedding Survival Guide

One advantage of marriage is that, when you fall out of love with him or he falls out of love with you, it keeps you together until you fall in again. – Judith Viorst

To keep your marriage brimming, With love in the loving cup, Whenever you're wrong, admit it; Whenever you're right, shut up. – Ogden Nash

If you want to sacrifice the admiration of many men for the criticism of one, go ahead, get married. – Katharine Hepburn

I'd marry again if I found a man who had fifteen million dollars, would sign over half to me, and guarantee that he'd be dead within a year. – Bette Davis

Never get married in college; it's hard to get a start if a prospective employer finds you've already made one mistake. – Elbert Hubbard

A good husband makes a good wife. – John Florio

Marrying an old bachelor is like buying second-hand furniture. – H. Jackson Brown, Jr.

When a man steals your wife, there is no better revenge than to let him keep her. – Sacha Guitry

For years my wedding ring has done its job. It has led me not into temptation. It has reminded my husband numerous times at parties that it's time to go home. It has been a source of relief to a dinner companion. It has been a status symbol in the maternity ward. – Erma Bombeck

Bachelors have consciences, married men have wives. – Samuel Johnson

Love: A temporary insanity curable by marriage. – Ambrose Bierce

Marriage is an adventure, like going to war. – Gilbert K. Chesterton

When a man opens a car door for his wife, it's either a new car or a new wife. – Prince Philip

Men have a much better time of it than women. For one thing, they marry later; for another thing, they die earlier. – H. L. Mencken

There is nothing nobler or more admirable than when two people who see eye to eye keep house as man and wife, confounding their enemies and delighting their friends. – Homer

The first time you marry for love, the second for money, and the third for companionship. – Jackie Kennedy

There were three of us in this marriage, so it was a bit crowded. – Princess Diana

Marriage is a series of desperate arguments people feel passionately about. – Katharine Hepburn

The true index of a man's character is the health of his wife. – Cyril Connolly

Source: http://www.frostmagazine.com/2014/05/quotes-about-marriage/

About The Author

Catherine married James in July 2014. They met in 2010 at Norbiton train station. They had a honeymoon baby and are now proud parents. They live in London. She is the founder and editor of Frost Magazine. She has been a writer for many years, having her first poem published when she was only 12-years-old. This is her second book, the first one was about acting. She is already working on number three.

She is also an actress and writes, produces and directs her own films.

Thank you to my family who were all there for me on the day, and on every other day of my life too. My parents, Helen and Bill and my brothers Peter and Steve. Thank you to my bridesmaids: Holly, Flora and Alexandra. Thank you to the leader of them all, Paloma, who was absolutely amazing. Thanks to Marcin. Thank you to my husband's family – now mine, too! – his parents and grandparents both helped. Thank you to everyone who came to the wedding. It was an amazing day and it was wonderful having you all there. Thank you also to our photographer, videographer and caterer. You were all first-class and made our day one of the best days of our life, despite all of the difficulties. Many thanks to Penelope Deacon and Margaret and Dick Graham: all encouraging and endlessly helpful. Thank you so much.

Printed in Great Britain
by Amazon

85772529R00098